Faith That Indigenizes

I remember very well the enthusiasm with which my dad spoke to me about the Power of God Church. He joined some of their packed services where he heard Pastor Luis Guachalla preach, listened to their radio station, and was impressed by their rapid growth. However, until I read this book, I never realized the importance of the Aimara background to understand the phenomenal growth of this denomination. Reading it also helped me to understand the Neo-Pentecostal background and the importance of globalization. Congratulations to my dear friend, Marcelo, and to the publishing house for publishing a book that touches on such a pertinent aspect of the Bolivian religious landscape.

Igor Amestegui
Former General Secretary of Bolivian Comunidad Cristiana Universitaria
Director of Langham Preaching Latin America

More than three million people in Bolivia and the western side of central South America speak Aimara, an ancient language and group of civilizations dating back more than two thousand years. The Aimara incorporate much ancient wisdom in their cultures regarding aspects of life like family social structures, agriculture, husbandry (llamas and alpacas), textiles, pottery, precious metals, and high-altitude survival. This book is unique as a casestudy of Aimara who have become members of the Neo-Pentecostal Power of God Church in Bolivia. Dr. Marcelo Vargas, a Bolivian pastor, theologian, and missiologist, is especially qualified to research, understand, and teach us regarding the interplay between ancient Aimara worldview and Neo-Pentecostal spirituality. He demonstrates how Aimara faith is shaping Bolivian Neo-Pentecostal life and how a Neo-Pentecostal spirituality interfaces, affirms, integrates, and strengthens aspects of ancient Aimara worldview, as understood by the Aimara themselves. This book is a must-read for anyone interested in issues of gospel and culture, acculturation, contextualization, the ancient wisdom of ancient people groups, Neo-Pentecostal Christianity, and pastoral issues facing immigrant peoples.

Charles Van Engen, PhD
Arthur F. Glasser Senior Professor Emeritus of Biblical Theology of Mission,
Fuller Theological Seminary, California, USA
Founding President and CEO,
Latin American Christian Ministries/ Programa Doctoral en Teologia PRODOLA

This study of Aimaran Neo-Pentecostals is an important contribution to understanding the persistence of indigenous spirituality, often classified by academics as "folk religion," or suspected by those tied to the cultural boundaries of western Christianity as "syncretistic."

Marcelo Vargas makes the compelling argument that the Aimaran religious worldview has always functioned continuously as a strong and stable substructure through all the adaptations and accommodations it has had to make in the face of Incan and Iberian Catholic incursions and, more recently, the global influence of classic Pentecostalism. While the Aimara Neo-Pentecostals share the emphasis on the miraculous and the suprarational, what has evolved is a vernacular version that empowers and transforms and at the same time solidifies and deepens Aimaran identity.

Those of us who are similarly negotiating the continuities and discontinuities between our primal cultures and the changes brought by European and American cultural emissions will resonate with the culture-specific, yet uncannily universal, insights of this book.

Melba Padilla Maggay, PhD
Chair, Institute for Studies in Asian Church and Culture (ISACC), Philippines

Faith That Indigenizes is an appropriate and telling title to Marcelo Vargas's book. It is the story of a historically subjugated people by various empires that resisted vigorously and sacrificially, maintaining their linguistic and cultural identity. It is a story of Aimara people making the gospel feel at home in their culture amidst the challenges of adapting to the city, poverty, marginalization, the new global realities, and the pilgrimage nature of the good news of the gospel. The study combines an emic approach with the analysis of the author, a Bolivian academic and mission practitioner, whose perspective enriches the study. I highly recommend its reading and welcome its publication to enrich our intercultural learning and mission encounters. This will be a valuable resource for mission oriented and theological institutions.

Rubén Paredes Alfaro, PhD
Dean, Programa Doctoral en Teologia PRODOLA

Marcelo Vargas's book, *Faith That Indigenizes: Neo-Pentecostal Aimara Identity*, presents a case study of Aimara involvement in the Power of God Church in La Paz, Bolivia. Three background chapters include the story of this megachurch that has become a religious phenomenon in La Paz. This leads to the specific case study where Vargas details why urbanizing Aimaras are attracted to the church. More significantly, he shows both how the church has changed the Aimaras involved and how the Aimara culture influences the church. While modifying some customs and demonstrating some western tendencies, such as greater individualism, Vargas argues that the underlying Aimara cultural values and worldview remain strong. This book should grace the shelves of any student interested in the integration of missiology, history, indigenous studies, and urban mission.

Nancy Thomas, PhD
Author of *A Long Walk, a Gradual Ascent: The Story of the Bolivian Friends Church in Its Context of Conflict* (2019)

Faith That Indigenizes

Neo-Pentecostal Aimara Identity

Marcelo Vargas A.

ACADEMIC

© 2022 Marcelo Vargas A.

Published 2022 by Langham Academic
An imprint of Langham Publishing
www.langhampublishing.org

Langham Publishing and its imprints are a ministry of Langham Partnership

Langham Partnership
PO Box 296, Carlisle, Cumbria, CA3 9WZ, UK
www.langham.org

ISBNs:
978-1-83973-587-5 Print
978-1-83973-704-6 ePub
978-1-83973-706-0 PDF

Marcelo Vargas A. has asserted his right under the Copyright, Designs and Patents Act, 1988 to be identified as the Author of this work.

All rights reserved. No part of this publication may be reproduced, stored in a retrieval system or transmitted, in any form or by any means, electronic, mechanical, photocopying, recording or otherwise, without the prior written permission of the publisher or the Copyright Licensing Agency.

Requests to reuse content from Langham Publishing are processed through PLSclear. Please visit www.plsclear.com to complete your request.

British Library Cataloguing-in-Publication Data
A catalogue record for this book is available from the British Library

ISBN: 978-1-83973-587-5

Cover & Book Design: projectluz.com

Langham Partnership actively supports theological dialogue and an author's right to publish but does not necessarily endorse the views and opinions set forth here or in works referenced within this publication, nor can we guarantee technical and grammatical correctness. Langham Partnership does not accept any responsibility or liability to persons or property as a consequence of the reading, use or interpretation of its published content.

Contents

Foreword xi

1   Introduction 1

2   Socio-Cultural Elements of Aimaran Identity 13

3   Bolivian Neo-Pentecostalism: Historical Context 41

4   The Power of God Church. 63

5   Aimaran Identity in the Power of God Church 89

Bibliography 121

Foreword

Families and individuals who have come to identify with Aimaran Neo-Pentecostalism have wrestled with the same challenges, idiosyncrasies, and competing expectations of a Eurocentric Christianity as those who have been proselytized and converted to other forms of Christianity in other colonized lands. The story is both new and old at the same time.

Critical questions emerge. How are we to make sense of our precolonial histories and cultures? Was everything that existed prior to the onslaught of colonization a vapour in the eyes of the Creator of the universe? What of the period of our lives under the influence of Catholic sponsored mission, itself often a reflection of colonial ideas, values, and practices?

Marcelo Vargas, in this small but pithy volume, walks us through the struggle to embrace authentic Christian faith by people of indigenous ancestry and context, seeking to maintain traditional indigenous identity. It matters little whether we're discussing Christianity in Uruguay, Paraguay, Chile, Bolivia, the USA, or Canada, the experiences are not overly different.

In a way that echoes Jaime Bulatao's "Split-level Christianity" and Paul Hiebert, Daniel Shaw, and Tite Tienou's "Excluded Middle,"[1] Marcelo draws us to the focal point of virtually all indigenous conversion stories: does one need to cease being indigenous to be Christian – Neo-Pentecostal or otherwise? And, if this is the case, how is life on this side of eternity to be understood – particularly considering the colonial experience?

It should not go unnoticed that Marcelo has flagged the very clear connection to indigenous ways of knowing, thinking, doing, and being – of tradition in all its facets and aspects – as needful for an authentic Aimaran Christianity.

By way of example, he notes that Aimaran Neo-Pentecostal power rituals identified in the faith practice and belief of the Neo-Pentecostal Power of God Church's (PoGC) converts have identifiable roots in Aimaran pre-Christian tradition. On the one hand, this suggests that they have yet to understand the

---

1. See: Jamie Bulatao, "Split-Level Christianity," *Philippine Sociological Review* 13, no. 2 (1965): 119-21; Paul G Hiebert, R. Daniel Shaw and Tite Tienou, "Responding to Split-Level Christianity and Folk Religion," *International Journal of Frontier Religion* 16:4 (Winter 1999/2000): 173-82; and Paul G Hiebert, "The flaw of the excluded middle." *Missiology* 10/1 (1982): 35-47.

middle ground of this present life, the period between birth and the afterlife, as lying in the sole domain of the Spirit of God. Instead, they hold somewhat fast to the notion that earthly power and ceremony must intercede since the heavenly cannot or does not. On the other hand, it also makes a strong case, as Marcelo himself does, that this is an authentic Aimaran expression of Christian faith, not an "Indigenous glossed" Western version imported or imposed in the land.

What's more, as Marcelo portrays PoGC Pentecostalism, he places the triumphs of the Aimaran indigenized Christian expression squarely and appropriately in the same class as adaptations made by the first followers of Jesus. It was, after all, here that the struggle to incorporate their new and vibrant experience of Jesus was realized. In the same way the early days of the church forced Gentile and Jewish believers to wrestle with culture and faith, Aimaran Christians are doing the same – engaging their oral and practiced traditions, long adhered to and pragmatically lived, as a fertile ground for Christian expression.

Whether it is the Acts 15 Council, or the demands of the Gentiles 150 years or so after; whether the cries from all quarters of the reformation, or the defiant actions of North American indigenous peoples, welcoming the authentic message of Jesus, all the while resisting the power of the colonial gospel – or the contemporary struggle of the Aimaran Neo-Pentecostals – the issue is and always has been the same. How does one make the Christian faith one's own? How does one share good news while eschewing cultural conversion?

With the church as a major force in colonization as a backdrop, Marcelo identifies individual agency, at times active community engagement, as central to the success of the gospel, no matter that the initial frame of reference within which Christianity was proffered was a colonial one. What's more, as with Lakota holy man Nicholas Black Elk in the USA or Mi'kmaw Sagamaw (Henri) Membertou in Atlantic Canada, the seed of the gospel was planted within them in such a way as to ensure their agency shaped the Christian experience to suit them and their culture, and not to placate the missionaries who sought to offer them instead, a Eurocentric potted plant.

Marcelo Vargas paints yet another in a series of decolonial portraits sketched by indigenous followers of Jesus, of the Spirit doing what only the Spirit can do: bring people alive in faith and culture without requiring them to choose one over the other!

Terry LeBlanc, PhD
Director, NAIITS: An Indigenous Learning Community
July 2022

1

Introduction

When in Time?

In approximately 800 BC a group of people living near Lake Titicaca, western South America, began to undertake a culturally distinctive form of life.[1] This indigenous cultural expression in the Andean region of Lake Titicaca legitimized social relations in time and space – customs, values, beliefs, and identity – within and between emergent Aimaran kingdoms.

The term, *Aimara*, comes from three words, *aya mara aru*, which together mean *language of the distant years*.[2] Although the origin of the Aimara is still a matter of scholarly debate, it is well known that the persistent, creative spirit of its people enabled them to endure despite two major outside invasions from the regionally dominant Inca Empire and the later European colonization that led to the Spanish Empire. These invasive periods were followed by another era during which Creoles – Spaniards born in Bolivia – ruled over the Aimara. When Bolivia became an independent Republic in 1825, the exploitation of the Aimara intensified rather than lessened.

The Aimaran identity is not simply a colonial or postcolonial replica of Incan and Spanish hybrid identity. It is rather a complex amalgam of features in which fundamental ethnic elements and foreign values co-exist. Aimaran people retain their language and autochthonous social, religious, political, and even economic structures due to their powerful sense of ethnic identity. The Spanish conquest, more than 500 years ago, was followed by constant, successive, territorial, social, and cultural intrusions but none of these could wipe out the Aimaran culture with its unique characteristics.

---

1. Beck, "Platforms of power," iii.
2. Llanque, *La Cultura Aymara*, 176; Estermann, *Filosofia Andina*, 9.

The strong emergence of the Aimaran identity seen today cannot be explained simply by referring to recent circumstances, such as the neoliberal policies that exacerbate extreme poverty or ongoing economic and cultural globalization pressures to make everyone identical in economic terms, and the social, political, and religious consequences these imply. History demonstrates the Aimaran people's long and tenacious struggle since pre-colonial times (when they were confronted with the Incas) to conserve and consolidate their ethnic and socio-political autonomy.

In recent times, particularly in the 1970s, the city of La Paz witnessed significant growth in the participation of Aimaran social actors in the quest to resolve poverty, exploitation, and discrimination. Urban and urbanized Aimaran residents appeared on the scenario as leaders who natively clarified their own aspirations, disseminated their hopes, and created a spreading mass movement based on Aimaran ethnic identity. There is no doubt that this indigenous movement has led to ethnic values, customs and traditions being much more highly appreciated today than by previous generations in Bolivia. Another undeniable outcome has been the democratic election of the country's indigenous vice president in 2021 – a man with Aimaran identity. All this contemporary socio-ethnic revolution was bound to have an impact not only on national life, but also on Neo-Pentecostal socio-religious phenomena.

Why Aimaran Identity?

As with the Neo-Pentecostals, Latin American Protestantism in general shows substantial growth and socio-cultural impact, giving rise to differing reactions and divergent interpretations. In many contemporary Catholic publications, according to Samuel Escobar, they are interpreted and described as a North American conspiracy and an invasion of sects. Escobar affirms: "If in the first stage, Protestant missionary action and presence were interpreted as part of a liberal-masonic-communist conspiracy, in its contemporary version the theory sees Protestantism as a part of a North American imperialist conspiracy."[3] From his Protestant roots, Escobar observes that the Catholics give a biased interpretation of the evangelical phenomenon.

Jean-Pierre Bastian, on the other hand, sees evangelical movements as showing syncretistic features that place them in a relation of continuity with traditional practices.[4] Bastian also argues that evangelicals are not authentically

---

3. Escobar, "Conflict of Interpretations," 117.
4. Bastian, Protestantismos y modernidad latinoamericana, 346.

Protestants as they practice their religion in a similar way to Catholics – both religions have their own form of syncretism.

Willems, D'Epinay, Martin and Stoll emphasize the social impact of Protestantism, particularly of Pentecostals, in Latin America.[5] Cook, Cox and Anderson, on the other hand, emphasize the religious impact.[6] However, all these authors agree that the identity of this socio-religious phenomenon contains much that is native and spontaneous. Pentecostals and Neo-Pentecostals contextualize their project in this part of the world with strength and spectacular growth.

Native cultures have stimulated the search for a clearer identity. In the study of the identity of the Maya people in Guatemala and in the state of Chiapas in Mexico, Virginia Garrard-Burnett says that the conversion to Protestantism is the final manifestation of the Maya strategy for adaptation and survival. She adds:

> However, I hope to make the case that, at least under some circumstances, this equation between Protestantism and Western ideology – the very notion of a "Protestant Ethic" – is our own cultural construction, which indigenous people have in some contexts effectively appropriated and reinvented for their own autochthonous purposes.[7]

Or as David Martin puts it:

> Whatever may be the truth about the pull of US power, it is evident that Pentecostalism (as well as other forms of evangelicalism) enables many of its followers to achieve a power in their lives which can simultaneously infuse them with the possibility of "betterment" and of new goods of every kind, spiritual and material, and also put them in touch with spiritual charges and discharges lodged deep in the indigenous culture, black, Indian or Hispanic. The long-term resources now drawn upon in people's lives run back both to the traditions of Protestant revival and to the ancient spirit worlds of Indian peasants and African slaves.[8]

---

5. Willems, *Followers of the New Faith*; D'Epinay, *El Refugio de las Masas*; Martin, *Tongues of Fire*; Stoll, *Is Latin American Turning Protestant?*

6. Cook, *New Face of the Church in Latin America*; Cox, *Fire from Heaven*; Anderson, *An Introduction to Pentecostalism*.

7. Garrad-Burnett and Stoll, *Rethinking Protestantism*, 1, 3.

8. Martin, *Tongues of Fire*, 204.

4   Faith That Indigenizes

Is this what is happening to the indigenous people when they become Neo-Pentecostals in Bolivia? How should Neo-Pentecostals be understood in the Bolivian context: as the front line of foreign penetration into the life of the nation, as a syncretistic combination of Protestantism and native religion, or as neither of these contrasting interpretations?

The growth of Protestantism is an important social phenomenon in Latin America today. The ethnic composition of the Bolivian people, including the evangelicals, is more homogeneous now because of the mass exodus of Quechuas and Aimaras to the eastern region of the country over the last thirty years, "… the Andean centrism of Bolivia has begun to bow before the evidence of the economic and demographic explosion of the East…".[9] Indigenous people from western Bolivia go east in search of land, work, and a better life. On leaving their native Andean highlands and associated lifestyle, they also leave the traditional Catholic Church. They join new churches that express with freedom indigenous values and traditional views and also support ethnic resistance and integration into new socio-religious practices.

The growth of the evangelicals in numbers, in their support from indigenous people, the roles granted to lay people and particularly women, and the aggressive style of evangelism practised, especially by Neo-Pentecostals, are factors that are transforming the religious scene in Bolivia. These changes in the social, political, and economic structure are dealing a harsh blow to the slavish feudal system imposed on the indigenous people who, as the majority group, are being given better conditions to throw off discrimination and come out of oblivion. They gain greater freedom of expression and action, and greater social, political, and economic mobility. Some take advantage of their new freedom to become union leaders but others opt to become evangelical church leaders. The greatest growth has occurred among the Aimara where it is the indigenous people themselves, rather than foreign missionaries, who exercise leadership roles.[10]

It is likely that, while contributing to Bolivian identity, evangelicals are also being shaped by it. The implantation of Protestant religion with Western roots has taken place within a specific cultural context, but the introduction of a new religion can neither exclude other religions nor replace them completely.

---

9. Mesa Gisbert, *Historia de Bolivia*, 137. The capital of the eastern Department of Santa Cruz, Santa Cruz de la Sierra, has multiplied its population since the 1970s thanks to thousands of immigrants from the western Andean region. According to the 1992 Census, 40.6% of the population of Santa Cruz are immigrants from other parts of Bolivia, with the number of immigrants growing by 182,0000 in the last 26 years. See Prado Meza, *Dios es evangelista no?*, 42.

10. Dussel et al, *Historia General*, 490.

How has the evangelical faith been presented, understood, and interpreted in the light of autochthonous beliefs and how – if at all – do these beliefs relate to the evangelical faith? What specifically is the relationship between native Aimara and present modern ways of life in the identity of the Power of God Church (PoGC) in La Paz?

The search for identity is an ongoing dilemma created by the massive social changes occurring both locally and globally. Any attempt to understand and keep up with social changes in the twenty-first century inevitably leads to questions about identity. Constant and apparently unending social change not only threatens long-standing institutions, but also the theories developed by social scientists considered to be experts in contemporary social mutations. On one hand, there are the technological changes and advances that affect telecommunications and biotechnology but, on the other, the emergence of indigenous people, who have historically been voiceless but who now have entered the world arena, is forcing the appreciation of new social paradigms that are implicitly cultural.

Western logic is based on dichotomies that, generally, compare two fixed values without contemplating the possibility of a third. Aimaran logic, like that of other ethnic groups in Africa, Asia and America, applies the principle of inclusion, even of opposites, leading sometimes to the relativization of absolute values.[11] The Andean world-and-life view contemplates additional values which do not exist in conflict but as complementary options – an identity lived in heterogeneity. Identity, therefore, cannot simply be defined in binary logical, rational, or intellectual terms. The relegated Aimaran identity has its own logic, which this study observes in its analysis of Bolivian Neo-Pentecostal identity.

Bolivian state structures in the past have marginalized indigenous groups because of their identity, relegated their indigenous languages, and rejected their traditional social forms. The same is true of their traditional community justice system and forms of transmitting indigenous identity to new generations.

Huge barriers have been built on the historic road walked by Bolivia's indigenous peoples – a road that has included several major milestones. The Spanish subjugated the peoples and cultures they found during their colonisation of South America. When the first Bolivian political constitution, written by Simon Bolivar, was approved 6 November 1926, and promulgated 19 November 1926, it was a constitution proposed by the Liberal party prioritizing state control. Although the first Constitution made an effort

---

11. Estermann, *Filosofía Andina*, 23, 141, 315.

towards structuring a modern state that avoided racial discrimination and slavery, the attempt failed completely.

The constitution maintained slavery and excluded the civil rights of most people born on Bolivian soil, leaving them at a disadvantage and completely vulnerable to discrimination based on their identity, history, and culture. Since the founding of the republic, the ruling elites have applied the state policy of controlling territories inhabited by indigenous people for their own benefit, meaning that they sacked and plundered property that did not belong to them. Even the 1953 Land Reform was based on the principle of *civilising the Indian*. On this subject, Colque and other authors write:

> The greatest effort to integrate the indigenous inhabitants of the Andes into Bolivian society was the implementation of the Education Reform after the 1952 Revolution with the intention of definitively inserting them into **modernity**. This line of thought, strongly influenced by the Mexican Revolution, opted for the cultural and social integration of the "Indian" into the **dominant culture**, seeking the disappearance of ancestral cultures.[12]

Bolivia is rather different to neighbouring countries, like Brazil and Chile, where the indigenous population is marginal, or even Peru and Ecuador, which have up to 25 percent indigenous population. Instead, Bolivia has a high percentage of indigenous people, both in rural and urban areas. The majority in Bolivia, two-thirds of the population, identify their ethnicity as indigenous.

The aggressions received throughout centuries of poly-ethnic coexistence have not quenched the Aimara's specific cultural identity. Indeed, it seems that constant hostility has strengthened that identity in many ways, deepening the meaning of being indigenous. The indigenous nature of the Aimara is experiencing nowadays a type of revival, particularly in its religious aspects.

The Aimara have suffered more than one or two hybridizations, whether socio-culturally with other cultures or in their religious world with groups like the Neo-Pentecostals. They have become a veritable melting pot of different cultural mixes throughout their existence. What is now recognized as the Aimaran culture was, at first, a mixture of different communities called *Aimara ayllus* that lived in the territory now known as Bolivia.

The Aimara have created an indispensable sense of being a people in order to trace the events of their history, their struggles, and their future.

---

12. Colque, "Identidad indigena, Nueva Constitucion Politica del Estado y desafios para la evangelizacion," 8

They have created through perseverance and suffering a cohesive force that has allowed them to both conserve and transform their ethnic identity. They have forged a new strength that binds them together and drives them forward – a strength based on their language, culture, tradition, and religion. They have integrated the cultural systems, production processes and religious thought of the national majorities. This is another factor that inspires an analysis of the Aimaran Neo-Pentecostals – to trace and find integration processes that make it possible to create conditions that lead, in turn, to greater justice and equity in Bolivian society.

Who Are Neo-Pentecostals?

The Neo-Pentecostals are a relatively new phenomenon in the Bolivian context and on the evangelical scene. They became established in Bolivia in the 1970s after a revival led by a Bolivian preacher called Julio Cesar Ruibal. Although they have Pentecostal origins and doctrines, with a few exceptions like the Comercio Street Congregation in La Paz, most have adopted dogmatic innovations, such as the prosperity gospel and an emphasis on spiritual warfare.

Neo-Pentecostals make extensive use of mass media communication and up-to-date technology. They are, in fact, a movement that has not only planted independent churches under national leadership, but whose influence now permeates all other denominations in their approach to worship and liturgy, especially among young people.[13] Neo-Pentecostals are the eager crowd that proselytize most and reach both poor and middle classes in Bolivia.

Neo-Pentecostalism succeeds in attracting large numbers of people in Bolivia, Latin America, and the world, controlling much more power and money than the original Pentecostal movement from which it arose. The Neo-Pentecostal movement also controls a significant number of radio stations and television channels. Their methodology includes a great capacity for innovation, which means that any members who miss church for one or two weeks run the risk of being left behind or feeling like outsiders when they return to church. New terminology and liturgy are frequently introduced and middle leadership, rituals, and ways of relating to the world outside are often revamped and changed. Charismatic leaders and their families control the Bolivian Neo-Pentecostal churches.

The magnetism of these leaders means that they create a personality cult and their church members are willing to obey their leader unquestioningly.

---

13. Berg and Pretiz, *Spontaneous Combustion*, 141

In addition to this dominant role, the Neo-Pentecostal leaders are centralising figures who focus all the spiritual powers, supernatural visions, decision-making, money management, and public relations on themselves. They leave no room for rivalry, feedback, or mistakes. A church is a true monolithic empire built to depend on and revolve around one person. Pentecostals have made their greatest impact in income-poor urban areas: the Brazilian favelas or shantytowns, Lima's so-called *young towns*, the *neighbourhoods of misery* in Buenos Aires.

In Bolivia, however, the indigenous Aimaras in the poor outlying areas of La Paz are being reached by the Neo-Pentecostal Church, specifically the Power of God Church (PoGC). This church makes an impact by doing miracle campaigns where healing miracles, often non-proven, are performed; and by broadcasting its services and campaigns via the mass media. This living Neo-Pentecostal phenomenon in La Paz at the PoGC carries within it a heart that beats with the blood of the indigenous Aimaran identity.

It should be mentioned that there are different versions of Neo-Pentecostalism and, to understand these differences, there is a need to be able to differentiate between classical Pentecostalism and Neo-Pentecostalism. Julio Córdova, a Bolivian sociologist, sees the nucleus of the religious experience as making the difference – classical Pentecostalism is more collective in nature while Neo-Pentecostalism tends to be individualistic. He also observes that the Pentecostal church exists almost exclusively in poor areas, while the Neo-Pentecostal movement also reaches middle class sectors of the population. He writes:

> Both phenomena imply a criticism of and adaptation to the modern world: Pentecostalism does so from an epistemological matrix that is basically "pre-modern" with its emphasis on community, and Neo-Pentecostalism does so from an epistemological matrix that is basically "post-modern" with its emphasis on the subjective, emotional individual.[14]

José Míguez Bonino, a Latin American Protestant theologian known for his incisive, broad-minded thought, calls the current Neo-Pentecostals *criollo Pentecostalism* or home grown Pentecostalism.[15] When he reflects on the piety and theology of Pentecostals, he makes a qualitative difference between classical and native Pentecostalism, linking the former to neoliberal

---

14. Córdova, "Tres ideas equivocadas sobre el movimiento neopentecostal," 112.
15. Bonino cited in Hansen, *El Silbo ecumenico del Espiritu*, 13.

economic policies generated by the dominant social classes and conditions in Latin America. Home grown Pentecostals tend to create administrative and doctrinal structures that are more vertical than the "social creation" within a predominantly local context made by the Neo-Pentecostals; vertical headship coalesces with a socialized management. Classical Pentecostalism, therefore, generates a type of rational adhesion that focuses on the "goods of religious consumption"[16], while native Pentecostalism attracts more emotional adhesions and focuses on empowerment.

Pentecostals, on the one hand, consider themselves to be Christians who are baptized with the Holy Spirit and receive spiritual gifts, for example, speaking in tongues (glossolalia), healing, and prophecy, but maintain their roots in Western missionary work. Neo-Pentecostals, on the other hand, are those who – in addition to having an intense Pentecostal experience of the power of the Holy Spirit accompanied by manifestations – also include spiritual warfare in their prayers, prosperity gospel in their teaching, independent structures, and more local roots and leadership in their organization. Indigenousness, historic background, theology, autonomy, forms of funding, and leadership style all combine to make Neo-Pentecostalism what it is today in Bolivia and Latin America.

This book gives a fair and frank appreciation to the native culture while also critically appreciating the globalized culture, with a view to obtaining a better understanding of the Neo-Pentecostal movement in Bolivia. The combination of local plus global lets ordinary people speak, allowing them to express and develop critical, vernacular paradigms about the secular social scientists and religious academics who have written about the movement. This is not a theoretical study based only in books and other people's thoughts and conclusions, but the conscious and/or unconscious perception and testimony of the authentic actors on the indigenized Neo-Pentecostal stage.

At first sight, Neo-Pentecostals from the Power of God congregations are blazing a trail for indigenous women to play leadership roles within a context of gender equity. They are also using their own language for services and adopting symbols and rituals that come from their own indigenous identity rather than Protestant tradition. Whether it is recognized or not, the Aimaran identity, not only in the PoGC, proposes new ways of living the Christian faith.

---

16. Bonino, *Rostros del Protestantismo Latinoamericano*, 59

Terminology

The definition of some important words for comprehending the arguments of this book follows below. The list of words is not exhaustive.

Worldview – This is understood to mean: the integral perception of the unseen and seen universe; the fundamental individual and collective orientation to life; the sensitivity to interpret the world and interact with it; that is, it is the spontaneous sense of existence based on beliefs. The concept in the English academic world is taken from the German philosophers' concept of *Weltanschauung* which is derived from *welt*, for world, and *Anschauung*, for perception.[17] There are abstract and non-abstract differences between worldviews. Cultures, societies and individuals each have an authentic worldview; consequently, there exists a variety of worldviews.

Culture – The Willowbank report defines culture as:

> "an integrated system of beliefs (about God or reality or ultimate meaning), values (about what is true, good, beautiful, and normative), customs (how to behave, relate to others, talk, pray, dress, work, play, trade, farm, eat, etc.), and institutions, which express these beliefs, values and customs (government, law courts, temples or churches, family, schools, hospitals, factories, shops, unions, clubs, etc.), which binds a society together and gives it a sense of identity, dignity, security, and continuity".[18]

Evangelical – This describes the individual, group, or church with a conservative view of fundamental Biblical doctrine, evangelistic passion, and missionary orientation with theology inherited from the sixteenth century European Reformation. The term also implies personal piety, puritan ethics, and global diversity. Protestants in Latin America prefer the name *evangelico* for historical reasons. The majority of the missionaries that came to preach were part of a special Protestantism; the fruit of their convictions and vocation were called evangelicals.[19]

Pentecostal – This describes churches, groups or individuals that have a great emphasis in the experience of the Holy Spirit manifested in speaking in tongues, prophecy, miracles, and healing. The movement that is called classic Pentecostalism is part of historical Protestantism. Pentecostal teaching has four cornerstones (a "foursquare gospel") that refer to four core beliefs: Jesus

---

17. Naugle, *Worldview: The History of a Concept*, xix, 64.
18. *Gospel and culture*, 3.
19. Escobar, "Que significa ser evangelico hoy?," 6–9.

Christ saves, heals, baptizes with the Holy Spirit, and is coming again. In Latin America, Pentecostal churches are deeply ingrained into two main lines: Pentecostalism as a result of the missionary work coming from North America and Europe, and Pentecostalism as a fruit of division from other traditional evangelical churches after a Pentecostal experience.

Neo-Pentecostal – This describes any person, church or group that has kept the classic Pentecostal spirituality but, in addition to being filled by the Holy Spirit, emphasizes new dimensions such as spiritual warfare, ecstasy in worship and/or unrestrained healing. They also have incorporated the prosperity gospel teaching. Christian faith means physical, emotional and spiritual success, and material prosperity. It is a non-denominational independent movement. Neo-Pentecostal churches in Bolivia were born independently from historical Protestantism in a revival that took place around the country under the leadership of Julio Cesar Ruibal at the beginning of the 1970s.

Globalization – This is "a historical epoch configured in the second part of the twentieth century, in which the convergence of economical, financial, communicational, and migratory processes increases the interdependency of vast sectors of many societies and generates new fluxes and supranational interrelations".[20] Globalization is more oriented towards markets than human beings and doesn't avoid inequality, racism, hybridism, and ethnocentrism. Globalization has liberating and oppressive features.

---

20. Garcia Canclini, *La globalización Imaginada*, 63.

2

Socio-Cultural Elements of Aimaran Identity

There have always been different forms of being Aimara, different ways of being indigenous in the city, in rural areas, in Eastern or Western Bolivia, in Northern Chile, in Buenos Aires, São Paulo, and Madrid. While acknowledging these diverse expressions, this chapter describes the socio-cultural religious elements that are the common denominator of Aimaran identity, that is, the features pertinent to Aimaras who have converted to Neo-Pentecostalism and those who have not.

Bolivia is an Andean country located in the centre of South America with no sea access, having given up its entire coastal territory to Chilean invaders during the Pacific War in 1879. It covers an area of 1,098,000 square kilometres and had a population of 11,145,770 inhabitants in 2017. The capital, La Paz, is the most culturally indigenous Latin American capital.

Of the Andean nations, Bolivia best preserves the indigenous identity inherited from the two most influential pre-colonial cultures of the region – Aimara and Quechua. People from these two cultures were part of the millions of New World inhabitants conquered subsequent to Christopher Columbus's landing in the Americas on 12 October 1492. Since the Genovese navigator, financed by the Spanish Empire, firmly believed he had reached Asian India, the indigenous people found on the continent were mistakenly called Indians – a term used still today. On referring to Bolivia, Herbert S. Klein says, "It is also the most Indian in the American republics: as late as the census of 1976 only a minority of the population were monolingual speakers of Spanish."[1] These precolonial cultures remain deeply rooted in most Bolivians despite a

---

1. Klein, *Bolivia: The Evolution of a Multi-Ethnic Society*, vii.

systematic opposition to their existence from the colonizing Spaniards and the Creoles of the Republican era.

The existing Bolivian Aimaran population live surrounded by mountains throughout the Altiplano (high plateau). They live in cities, such as La Paz, and in rural communities sprinkled across this broad plateau. The plateau reaches an altitude of 4000 metres. It covers almost 1,000 kilometres from north to south, includes the Lakes Titicaca and Poopo, and reaches to the Uyuni and Coipasa Salt Flats on the western side of Bolivia.

The Aimara, more than other indigenous groups, have given Bolivia a firm sense of geographical and cultural belonging, providing a sense of national identity amidst all the diversity found within its borders. The Bolivian identity and conscience are indigenous and this is the profound, true root of national identity even today, just as the Latin American continent is also Indo–American.

In addition to this background, the Aimara have been affected by new and numerous impacts in the last century.[2] They have been moulded by political, social, economic, and religious influences and changes. Modernity and globalization have hit them with all their force via education, democracy, legislation, and trade unions. Non-Catholic religious groups and the proliferation of new forms of Christianity has brought new sources of tension and profound changes. Evangelical Protestant denominations have made inroads into Aimaran indigenous communities, none with more success than the Neo-Pentecostals, although these, just like previous invasions, have failed to erase the fundamental components of Aimaran ethnic identity.

The Distinctive Nature of Aimaran Culture

What are the common characteristics of Aimaran culture, regardless of beliefs? How can we analyse the specific context of Aimaran Neo-Pentecostal believers? This chapter will discuss different aspects of Aimaran culture, including Aimaras' worldview, indigenous spirituality, language, multi-ethnic sense, three-dimensional logic, and integral epistemology.

Worldview and Spirituality

What do the Aimara think about themselves and about the world? How do they perceive who they are and the world around them? How do they conceive the spiritual and material worlds?

---

2. Albó "La experiencia religiosa Aymara," 83.

The great obstacle when trying to respond to these questions is that our effort to understand these issues tends to be monocultural: in other words, people try to mould indigenous understanding based on the modern Western paradigm. This paradigm tends to conceive life as divided into separate, independent compartments; although this attitude may be gradually changing, it still tends to be dominant. Doing so impoverishes reality. The mindset of the native Aimara conceives life in a way that is different from, and often contrary to, the Westernized mindset. Life and the world, for Aimara, are an integrated whole that is fundamentally spiritual and in harmony with the cosmos. For example, the passing of time is always associated with places. Both are perceived as inseparable.

One Aimara word that expresses the unity between time and space and the complementarities between them is the word, *pacha*. Pacha is the simultaneous expression of two forces: space and time, or in Aimara/Quechua worldview "sacred time and space, history, existence."[3] This is seen, for example, in the *Pachamama*[4] concept which literally means "mother space and time" but is commonly understood to mean Mother Earth. The term evokes ideas that refer not only to earthly matter but also to the time lapsed in it, including what surrounds that cannot be seen – the invisible spiritual world.

Pachamama simultaneously includes spiritual and material realities that are shared by human beings, animals, plants, and spirits. For the Aimara, everything is sacred – inert material as much as animals and human beings. Everything that exists and moves in the environment is classed as spiritual. The mountains, the earth, the rivers, the rocks – all of these are full of spirits: *achachilas*[5], *awichas*[6], the Pachamama, and other inferior protective divinities belonging to the ancestors. The spirits inhabiting these places can be beneficial, but they may also be harmful. Once dead, human beings – both male and female – become incorporated into the spiritual world that coexists with the visible world.

There are three worlds or three levels intimately related to one another. In these three dimensions can be found both the natural and the supernatural realms that are invisible, but very real. The *aka pacha, the concrete world of life,*

---

3. Estermann, *Teologia Andina*, 483.

4. *Pachamama*, Mother Earth is the most important female Aimaran divinity. At the same time personifies the fertility of the earth and is worshiped as a protector of all men. Strobele-Gregor, *Indios de piel blanca*, 330.

5. *Achachilas* are the tutelary and ancestral spirits that protect the Andean communities.

6. *Awicha* literally *grandmother* in the Aimara language, the ancestral spirit that becomes flesh in the fire. Estermann, *Teologia Andina*: 473, 475.

is related to forces from below and above; *manqha pacha*, the world below, with its superior powers and *alajj pacha, the world above,* is linked to the concept of heaven. It would be a mistake to equate this trilogy with the Christian understanding of earth, hell, and heaven or with human beings, the devil and God.

Where would the spirits be in this three-dimensional diagram? They are everywhere. Good and evil spirits or divinities are intermingled and present in each dimension. This belief, which divides the cosmos into three levels, is a crude systematization of the original Aimaran understanding. It is an adaptation of the original indigenous concepts with Roman Catholic concepts.

How do the Aimara understand their world and fit into it? With the arrival of Christian spirituality and morality, a foreign worldview was incorporated into Aimaran metaphysical outlines. It was an adaptation that, on the one hand, left their own continuities alive and, on the other hand, strengthened them. However, inevitably, changes and modifications occurred which, in turn, became apparent in their own discontinuities. For example, the Western worldview makes a clear opposition and separation between heaven and earth while, for the Aimara even today, the alajj pacha and the manqua pacha have mixed elements of wickedness and kindness. Not all the bad is in the manqua pacha (hell) neither is all the pure in the alajj pacha (heaven). Although there are forces that work for wrong, these same forces can work for good, and this is part of the framework of the belief and morality of the ancient Aimara.

Social Life: Multicultural and Intercultural

Under which norms of life do the Aimara live? What are their more esteemed cultural values? All ethnic groups set their modus vivendi according to the worldview, needs, problems, and experiences they have had throughout their history. In community life, the *ayllu* is an ancestral base of coexistence; Aimaras in the city have urbanized adapted versions of this coexistence. It is the mutual adhesion between the individual and his or her own community, without forgetting the aspect of nature. It provides security and sociability. Solidarity is the spirit of life in the community where the good or the harm committed by the individual affects the entire community. Reciprocity, the *ayni*, reflects the belief that all forms of help received must be rewarded with generosity and commitment. Spiritual holism between the individual, the community, and the cosmos surrounds the culture in everything; the sacred is to be found both in daily life and in major ritual events.

The interrelationships found in each event and in the Aimaran personality are a vital foundation for their identity. In the Aimaran conscience, however, the human being is not the centre. Man and woman are not considered in an isolated or individualized form. Nature and the cosmos coexist, they feed each other, and they protect and mutually respect each other. Community life is where needs, preferences, and a sense to life are generated. The human being is inserted into the physical and spiritual atmosphere that surrounds him or her to form one indivisible entity. It is impossible to live without the diverse fabric and multifaceted nature of interdependent cosmic relationships. However, not everything is perfect in the Aimaran ayllu. Community life, be it in the rural or urban context, combines highly humane values with less ethical levels of domination, harmful perversion, and denigrating discrimination. A mixture of desirable values and anti-values can be found in the collective lives of native people.

Aimaran creativity is expressed with a sense of originality: their sense of festiveness is also expressed in the logic of celebration and their interdependence is expressed in reciprocity and complementarity. However, there are also shadows of fatalism in which fate is stained with pessimism and accommodation to the belief that natural and supernatural forces are pig-headed and unavoidable. Frivolity, cheating, and vengeance are seen as acceptable forms of behaviour: despair is commonplace because life is seen only in terms of the present with few positive roots in the past or indications of a better future.[7]

Language

The Aimaran culture is a relational culture. Its channels and its sources are not written documents produced by individuals. The Aimara do not determine tradition by conceptualizing or idealizing their utopias in written texts. The Aimara's main "text" is a colourful fabric of live perceptions in minds and hearts. It is a treasure of accumulated community wisdom, shared by means of an oral ancestral tradition, and manifested in beliefs, customs, and forms of life. Rather than being textual, Aimaran communication has been and still is a living experience. As a result, language is central to Aimaran culture.

Aimara as a language gives its speakers an abundance of linguistic resources. It is enough to know some of the grammatical system to have a clear idea of the wealth and complexity of this language. The extensive

---

7. Tancara, *Teologia Pentecostal*, 5. Thomas 1998, *Weaving the Word*, 256.

demarcation of the sources of information, the affirmation of humanity, the linguistic differentiation of humanity from the non-human, and the dynamic interaction between language, culture and the perception of the world are also aspects of the Aimara language. Neither the Aimaran culture or its language is gender-biased towards the use of masculine nouns or pronouns as in Spanish and English. When an Aimara speaks about human beings, he or she does not exclude half the human race by referring to someone only in masculine terms. The language, with derivations in the culture, gives the Aimaran woman an equal social level in terms of gender and justice.

The inclination in other languages to one gender focus is neutralized in the Aimara language by a preference for using the second person. Spanish and English tend to give priority to the first person, leading inevitably to a degree of individualism. But the relational values of the Aimara give the balance against any kind of selfish chauvinism. The use of "you" instead of "I" makes gender equality and harmony work.

Three-Dimensional Logic

Implicit within the language is a tripartite logic.[8] The logic of Aimaran thought is not dichotomous. In other words, it is not conclusive or absolutist on one hand, and static and centred in the individual on the other. It does not have the binary logic of belief or non-belief, or the legitimization of a unique, exclusive, closed system of beliefs. This tripartite logic implies the compassionate submission to Aimaran religious community life and its syncretistic practices, but at the same time, the construction of elements that modify the established pantheon.

The Aimaran world-and-life view starts in the same way as the Vedic tradition of India – in the non-duality of reality.[9] Reality is not conceived in dimensions that are in conflict or opposed to each other such as good and evil, sacred and profane, masculine and feminine, visible and invisible, true and false. Both realities coexist. God exists and so does the devil; human beings and nature coexist; likewise, spirit and body. In the Aimaran concept of cosmos, there is room for a third alternative of equal importance. The parts do not attack each other; on the contrary, they are complementary, inclusive.

It is typical for Aimara not to polarize reality between good and evil, but to mediate between positive and negative forces. A rich Aimaran oral narrative, the well-known story about "The fox that went to heaven", illustrates

---

8. Lozada, *Identidad y vision del mundo Aymara*, 10.
9. Estermann, *La filosofía andina como alteralidad que interpela*, 6

a non-dualistic logic. Thomas analyzes the story deeply into social Aimaran normative rules and its incidence in oral communication.[10] The tripartite sense of the universe is evident in stories like this. Another way to understand it is as "intentional ambiguity". Tolerance of ambiguity has an effect of conciliation between wrong and right, order and disorder, individual and communal, heaven and earth, and between religious and social grounds. Intentional ambiguity was part of the historic encounter with the Catholic religion and is very much alive in encounters with modern religions similar to Neo-Pentecostalism.

Inadequate Western Moulds

The concepts and methodology of Westernized rationality, therefore, are inadequate and limited for outlining the depth of the distinctiveness of Aimaran culture and other cultures that have a holistic nature. Applying preconceived presuppositions that determine our narrow understanding under Western systems cannot do justice. The classic definitions of terms like worldview, identity, culture, and religion have imposed limited boundaries that cannot embrace the fullness of what the Aimara are and believe today.

The distinctive character of Aimaran identity invites a responsible paradigmatic change that may place researchers outside Western centrism; it does justice to the qualitative equity of all ethnic identities thus revealing desires, which are often subtle and concealed.

Is the Neo-Pentecostal experience at the PoGC specifically and profoundly Aimaran? Do their principles, values, sacred holism, cosmic interrelationship, orality, linguistic inclusivism, three-dimensional logic, and thirst for the unknown place them outside pure and inadequate Western moulds or inside their intentional ambiguity?

Integration: The Concept of Pacha

The concept of pacha implies considering not just the human neighbour (without the common current chauvinism), but also nature and the cosmos.

---

10. Thomas, *Weaving the Word*, 228–247. A summary of the story is: A fox wanted to go to heaven; it took a lift with a condor. They attended a mass served by God the Father; after that, they went to eat in a garden with all kinds of fruits. The fox ate a lot and asked the condor to wait for long time. Becoming tired, the condor left without him. Puzzled by this, the fox made a rope and began to climb down. On the way back down, he insulted parrots which then bit the rope in two. The fox fell and died. His stomach split open and the seeds within scattered, making earth fertile especially in the East.

The Aimara language did not have one concept for time and another concept for space, but integrated the two concepts.

Time was – and is – not conceived without space or space without time. The word, pacha, as mentioned before, includes simultaneous and inseparable concepts of time and space. In fact, the meaning of this expression is much richer, not only because it integrates time and space but all the subjects of reality. The pacha includes plants, animals, water, stones, earth, human beings, stars, sun, moon, etc.; the pacha integrates the life of the whole cosmos. Pacha means the encounter and interaction of all the living, active contributors of reality and existence itself. Because the environment is imbued with spirituality, every seen and unseen being is sacred and capable of feeling. Nature feels, as do animals, human beings, and spirits. Feeling the cosmos is pacha.

This broad vision of history and associated space was diffused because of the wide territorial mobility of the Aimara. Aimaras shared their territories, spreading westwards from the central nucleus of what is now the Bolivian Andes to the Pacific Ocean and eastwards to the Amazonian tropical rainforest. The effort to consistently preserve the Aimaran character inherited from the forefathers explains the cultural persistence still shown by the Aimaran people today.

The territorial boundaries of the Aimara mean they had access on the western side to the Pacific Ocean to obtain sea products, and on the eastern side to the valleys and tropical forests that provided fruit and vegetables native to those regions. These so-called traverse fringes of the mountainous block gave access to a variety of ecosystems that linked the Altiplano and mountains with the coast and tropical forest.[11] Their locale beside sea, mountains, and jungle suggests two things: the different Aimaran kingdoms interacted with nature and natural resources wisely; and, because the kingdoms many times intermixed, the kingdoms maximized their capacity to take advantage of their resources by sharing them.

Community and Social Life

The traditional worldview, unavoidably associated with natural forces, continues to be valid today, both in the countryside and in the city. It was maintained because of the ethnic continuity, and it has created an elemental symbolic Aimaran community which is still found in the perception of life held by members of the PoGC congregations. The Aimaran worldview today

---

11. Platt, "Pensamiento politico Aymara," 365-450.

maintains the rich, constructive values of reciprocity and communal life among rural and urban people. However, as occurs to people from all cultures and conditions, Aimaras in the PoGC face some tough issues. Church members tend to respond to the attitudes of familiar and non-familiar sources with hatred and vengeance, reproducing attitudes of discrimination against children and women, and falling into the common cultural pitfall of ethnocentrism. Carter and Mamani sum up the Aimaran worldview concisely in two words – "negative fatalism."[12]

The balance between natural and supernatural forces is expressed in frequent religious festivals held in a context of misery and marginalization. Alcoholism is widespread with its consequences on family, children, and increased poverty. The values already highlighted, inherited from ancient times, such as reciprocity, complementarity, and community life regulate relations to promote the common good. They are deep-rooted but defective. They have shown themselves to be sustainable in building the Aimaran sense of the supernatural and the will to fight for Aimaras' freedom and culture, but the Aimaras are still building their identity. They are developing their own style, combining their own shapes and colours. It is a mistake for Neo-Pentecostals to think that they are unique to current times. Similarly, scholars of the Aimaran phenomenon are wrong when they focus on a glorious Aimaran past, uninfluenced by the West, and when they ignore Aimaran roots which contribute much to Aimaran identity.

Criticism of Westernization

A review of more than 120 years of Protestant missionary work in Bolivia recognizes that the missionaries and the church are far from the indigenous reality. They have moulded their work more to Western identity than biblical foundations, grassroots identity, or the lessons learnt from history. Various authors from the northern and southern hemispheres have observed direct and indirect parallels between missionary development and the expansion of Western modernism, as much in concept as in method. Nowadays, those who promote Western individualistic values are no longer the conservative foreign missionaries, but Bolivian pastors who have adopted foreign theologies and lifestyles which supposedly offer more intelligent and wealthy modes of life. This error has taken a toll in terms of institutionalized superficiality, the violation of cultural identity, and a denial of the most precious evangelical values.

---

12. Carter and Mamani, *Irpa Chico*, 365.

Currently, the Aimara as an ethnic group and culture live in the large territories they have occupied since pre-colonial times – in the Bolivian and Peruvian highlands and the northern coastal region of Chile. But the Aimara are not static and the new generations who have moved to the cities are changing. As a result, the strong social contemporary movement to revindicate Aimaran rights has arisen not from the Aimaran rural communities, but in the urban centres among factory or mining workers, and in trade unions and neighbourhood associations.

Bolivian Aimaras in the cities of La Paz, Oruro, Potosí, Cochabamba, and Santa Cruz or in foreign cities such as Buenos Aires, Lima, Arequipa, and Tacna, or in Moquegua, Iquique, and Arica do not lose their identity.[13] They are people with their own distinctive customs and beliefs. They do not tend to be moulded by the characteristics of their environment.

As we analyse the Aimaran people and culture within their dynamics of change within the religious, social, demographic, and intellectual realms, we see that Bolivians are witnessing a resurgence of Andean ethnicity in general and Aimaran ethnicity in particular. In the face of the ideological trends prevalent at the end of the twentieth century and beginning of the twenty-first century, the Aimara have seen the need to meditate on their role and defend their identity and values. Today, all of us have witnessed the emergence of ethnic native movements in different parts of the world: Chechens and Ukrainians in the former Soviet Union; Croatians and Bosnians in the former Yugoslavia; Catalans and Basques in Spain; Tutsis and Hutus in Rwanda; Aimaras and Quechuas in Bolivia. It seems this is the time for reaffirming ethnic identities all over the world. Perhaps this is a way of counter-balancing the invasion of globalization. The power of nations and ethnic groups does not lie in their territorial limits or their economy, but in their character and identity.

Not all the Bolivian population is Andean, just as not all those who live in the city of La Paz are Aimaran. However, the whole population can be considered as culturally Andeanized. It would be a mistake to ignore the Aimaraization of the Creole and *mestizos paceños* (people from La Paz) because people from all social classes perform and participate in the religious venues, same rituals, and folklore. The same Aimara religious agents, the *yatiris*,[14] offer

---

13. Llanque, *La cultura Aymara*, 179; Albó, *Raices de America*, 31.

14. *Yatiri* in Aimara language literally means *the one who knows* or teacher. He is the community priest, a ritual specialist. His special powers do not come from the community nomination but from supernatural powers selection make evident by being reached by a ray. Surviving the experience of being hatched by a ray gives spiritual authority. Albó, *Raices de America*, 480.

their services to middle class intellectuals, rich entrepreneurs, politicians, and poor natives. The religious belief has been Aimaraized, while those without religion see the culture being clothed in an Aimaran identity.

These observations may surprise many because it is often assumed that the Aimaran religion has been Westernized. A closer analysis, however, of the collective worldview and the system of symbols found in the different aspects of modern Bolivian life reveals an increasingly indigenous identity in the country as a whole and a strong Aimaran influence in the highland region (Altiplano) and beyond.

A Particular Way of Living and Perceiving the World

The indigenous worldview, essentially different from the Western one, exercises a powerful influence in Bolivian society, defining the religious and social behaviour of the majority. Despite the introduction of foreign rituals and customs, Bolivian Neo-Pentecostal Christianity has not completely replaced indigenous religiosity. The advance of Neo-Pentecostalism is taking place specifically in the Aimaran cultural context in the city of La Paz, without eliminating or replacing other existing religions in a similar mode as in Africa. The indigenous Aimaran identity still builds values, behaviour, and religiosity in Bolivia. All evangelicals, particularly Neo-Pentecostals, are strongly influenced by the indigenous worldview.

Neo-Pentecostal Mission towards Quechuas and Aimaras

Global transformations and the loss of myths have changed the religious panorama in Bolivia. Just as the indigenous social movements have unmasked the myth of a homogenously mixed nation, evangelicals have dismantled the traditional idea of a uniformly Roman Catholic population. Much more so than the Quechua, Aimaran evangelicals question the dominant socio-religious system because they insist that indigenous people from the poorest sectors of society achieve a greater sense of identity and dignity.

A joint history and territorial context have created a bond between the Aimara and Quechua peoples. Both have many comparable ethnic, geographical, and historical aspects, differing apparently only in terms of language. Centuries of development side-by-side in the Bolivian Andes have increased the similarities and accentuated the differences.

The Quechua rule over the Aimara occurred when they spread to the south of Cuzco, the capital of the Inca Empire, in the thirteenth century before the Spanish colonization. Initial attempts to use force did not last long and Quechua groups opted to adopt a peaceful strategy and moved to Aimaran territories led by an Inca representative. With a view to breaking the unity of the Aimara, the Quechua settled in the Bolivian Andes, first around Lake Titicaca before moving down to the warmer valleys. This was the start of the correlation between the two cultures, which today, after seven centuries of exchange and coexistence, represents the main foundation for Bolivian's identity.

An ethnic-comparative analysis of the penetration of modern religious offers such as Neo-Pentecostalism among the Quechua and Aimara reveals two different routes: one of flexibility and the other of resistance. The Quechua have taken a more open historical course. Their very origins have much more hybrid elements, they have succeeded in coexisting with other cultures, they have spread further afield, and this has given rise to greater interdependence. The Aimara, on the other hand, have been more culturally closed and geographically static – they have resisted hybridism and cultural mixing. As a result, their cultural identity, despite being as dynamic and changing as any culture must be, has been less influenced by religious incursion.

The encounter of the Aimara with evangelical religiosity has not changed this historical pattern. The Aimara hold on to their ethnicity tenaciously, building a new Neo-Pentecostal identity, which is still based on their indigenous world-and-life view.

The evangelical modus vivendi, which remains imprisoned by a set of ideas about God and Jesus Christ, combined with a few spiritual disciplines like prayer but without opening itself up to the non-rational dimension of life, has no chance of reaching deep into the spiritual hunger of Neo-Pentecostal Aimaras.

Traditional Aimaran Religion: Structure, Deities, Rituals and Specialists

Have the Aimara retained their pre-Catholic deities, rituals, and religious specialists throughout their long religious history or has pre-colonial religiosity been completely annulled? Guaygua and Castillo say that there is a juxtaposition of religious logic between popular Catholicism and Aimaran beliefs.[15] Does a similar juxtaposition exist between Neo-Pentecostals and Aimaras? It would not be wise to make affirmations about Aimaran religiosity without having a clear idea of what that religiosity implies. Therefore, this chapter gives a

---

15. Guaygua and Castillo, *Identidades y religion*, 39.

brief description of traditional Aimaran religion – its structure, deities, rituals, and specialists.

The starting point for this analytical description is the testimonies collected during fieldwork. The subjects are members of the Neo-Pentecostal PoGC. Three testimonies have been selected from sixty that raised some revealing aspects of perceptions moulded by the past. These stories show that the beliefs of the traditional Aimaran religion are not completely – or even partially – eliminated.

> My mother used to tell me about a lady whose face was hurting and that gave her a headache. A yatiri came and, in a closed room without light, started to pray. Then a kind of wind came and the yatiri began to hit the air with his belt and ask in Aimara where the spell was and then you could hear some voices but only he could understand. Afterwards they went out and in the stable where cows were fed, they found a stake where toads and small lizards were almost dying with pins, hair, and underwear belonging to the lady. He released them saying that if the small animals died, the lady would also die…Yes, these things work, at least for a period of time.
>
> For example, I am going to tell you about my mum. My mum died eight years ago. She died of alcohol poisoning and for eight days we did the things you're supposed to do: drinking alcoholic drinks and during those eight days we burned her clothes, everything there was, the newer things we kept and the oldest stuff we burned. Then we wore black for a year and after that we stopped wearing black – we had a party and a bonfire. We jumped over the bonfire. I think your sorrow and I don't know what else gets left in the bonfire.
>
> A yatiri came to my house; three and half years ago my aunt had a clothing shop. Then he starts healing each one in the family so as to change their luck, because maybe someone might have been under a curse, and then he starts one by one. Then somebody gave a paper wrapped up to put near to the heart, after that he knelt and started singing in Aimara and with incense. The following day he gave us some liquid to throw out near another lady's shop so that she would pass on her luck to us when we stepped on the liquid, but we could also make a little hole in the ground near to

another shop and put in a small tied-up packet to receive her/his luck.

The first testimony, which belongs to a young man who is not a new convert to Neo-Pentecostalism, opens a window to see the worldview of the Aimara. The voices heard are understood to be spirit voices. The second testimony belongs to a young woman who has also attended the PoGC for some time. She introduces us to the universe of rituals, describing some of the rituals offered for the dead. The third is another long-term male PoGC member who gives us a glimpse of what could be called the Aimaran religious specialists, the most accepted of which is the yatiri.

Structure

Sacredness is the raw material that lies at the heart of the Aimaran culture. It is unacceptable for any Aimaran person not to believe in God and the deities, or to try to remove the Catholic Christian images, content, and symbols from their rituals, even though these latter elements were forced upon their ancestors with the arrival of the Spanish. Aimaran men and women have a religious attitude to life and see all their activities as having a spiritual significance. This results in a complex system of rituals linked to the agricultural calendar and Catholic saints' days, which were introduced in the sixteenth century.

The perception of a supreme being, both as the *Apu Kollana Auqui* who is the Sovereign Father God and *Wiracocha* who is God, the creator and cultivator of this Earth, is found in Aimaran religiosity.[16] They believe that he is the creator who protects everything that exists and is the human beings' benefactor. However, they also see him as a distant, inaccessible god, who lives in paradise, from where he is always ready to punish.

He communicates via natural phenomena and special human and non-human envoys. The Aimaran people also recognize the existence of other spiritual beings that have power, but nothing compared to God's power. Some are called "tutelary" or protector spirits, which means that the people do good and give offerings to win the favour of these spirits. Other spirits, however, are considered to be evil spirits who exist to do evil; once a spell or curse has been made, it can only be countered by giving a series of offerings to the evil spirit.

The Aimaran belief system includes deities who are do-gooders; their vital force is found in nature and the cosmos. These deities vary depending

---

16. Jolicouer, *El Cristianismo Aymara*, 34.

on the geographical region, but most are situated in the Andean aka pacha, mentioned before as one of the three spaces of their worldview. They can also be in the alajj pacha, the world above.

Deities

Tutelary Spirits

Some Aimaran deities that date back about five centuries have resisted being displaced by Christianity. In many cases, the Aimaran belief system has merged with the Christian belief system, legitimizing the performance of the Aimaran belief system's functions. In other cases, it has assumed new "Christian" functions, baptizing ancient deities with a new name even though they maintain a strong ancestral identity. As a result, a Bolivian Christianity without Aimaran religiosity is unthinkable, as is an Aimaraism without Christianization.

The Aimaran perception of reality sees mountains, lakes, rivers, land, rocks, and other facets of nature as having a spirit, a will, and the capacity to act. Every part of nature and its products possess spirits, even those that result from human work and art. An Aimara seeks to feel the powerful spiritual force of the cosmos and nature around him and sees life in all his surroundings, both in human and non-human beings. In this kind of indigenous spirituality, the tutelary spirits or guardians/tutors, offer protection, but only if their "hunger" is satisfied. If not, they can feel offended, become angry and cause harm, just as an evil spirit would.

1. Pachamama

The most widely known and worshiped of the tutelary spirits is the Pachamama or mother earth, also called the *wirjina*, which clearly identifies her with the virgin Mary. She represents geographical space, time, and movement, and includes natural resource and cropland. In urban areas, the land where houses are built belongs to the Pachamama. The Aimara believe that this tutelary spirit gives life to the crops, fertility to the soil, and food to her sons and daughters, the humans. The Pachamama is both one and many, present everywhere, even in the most rugged, dangerous areas. She protects and punishes, is a generous provider, but is easily angered. She must be fed if you want to be fed and protected if you want protection. Her name is Pachamama because the earth is like a mother. This belief reflects the strong affection for the land since it is there that all humans are born, eat, live, and die. The Pachamama may appear in the form of a woman and speak with a woman's voice, but she may also take the form of a toad.

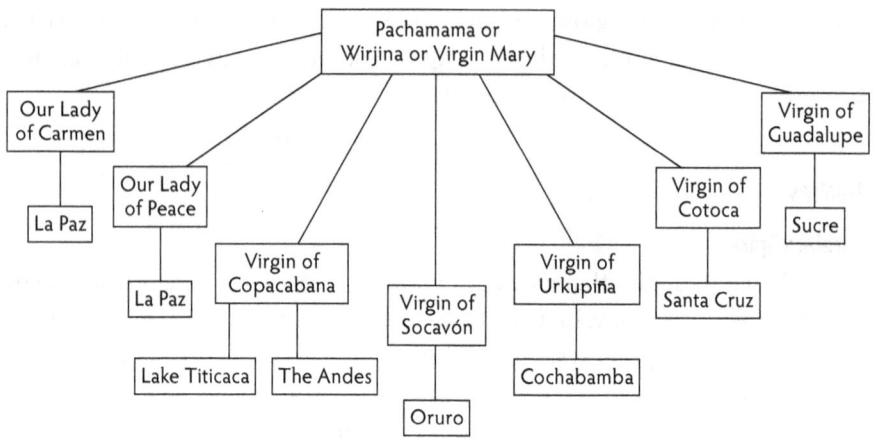

Figure 1: Taxonomy of Pachamama and Roman Catholic Syncretism in Various Places

2. Achachila

This name comes from the Aimaran word, *achachi*, which means grandfather or ancestor, and refers to the belief that every high or steep place has a spirit. The spirits of the mountains and hills, called *achachilas*, *wak'a*s or *achilas*, take care of the hill itself, the community living there, and the wider region. They teach how to live well and in harmony with the cosmos and are named after the hills and mountains in the area. They are the lords of the clouds, rain, hailstones, snow, and water and are capable of becoming angry and dishing out punishment. The spirits of the most important ancestors receive the names of the highest mountains; for example, *tata Illimani* and *tata Illampu*, which protect large areas such as whole regions, are the most powerful spirits. Most of these spirits are masculine.[17] In contrast, the lesser ancestors, the *jisk'a achachilas*, are found in lower, more accessible hills; these do the same job for smaller territories and for each ayllu. The achachila may appear in human form or in dreams. Catholic saints have been included among these tutelary spirits; it is believed the saints protect those who worship them by praying to them or by holding patron saints' day festivals.

3. Iqiqu or Ekeko

This is the tutelary spirit of abundance, fertility, and happiness. He is worshipped particularly at the summer solstice in January when a craft fair is

---

17. Spedding, *Religión en los Andes*, 110.

held in La Paz called *Alasita* (which means "to buy"); this is the celebration dedicated to the *ekeko*. This tutelary spirit is always represented as a small, fat man, with mestizo features, carrying all kinds of things, particularly domestic appliances. (Mestizo people have mixed ancestry with both white European and indigenous backgrounds.) The belief is that he scares away misfortune while attracting abundance and good luck. He has a round hole in his mouth because he enjoys smoking cigarettes, and he also likes to drink alcohol. The miniatures sold at the Alasita fair represent what each person wants in their life: a house, a car, a lorry, a baby, a university degree, an air ticket. After the miniatures have been offered to the Iqiqu or Ekeko, they are taken to a Catholic church where the priest also blesses them.

4. Kuntur Mamani

The *Kuntur Mamani* protector spirit is mostly associated with the roof of the house, which appears to be why its name means "condor hawk" (condors and hawks being two of the birds most revered by the Aimaras). However, this spirit's realm goes beyond the roof and includes the entire house and the family living in it. The feminine part is the *qhiri awicha*, which means "kitchen grandmother" and refers not only to the kitchen, but also to the home itself. Everything associated with the domestic scenario is included in the area protected by this spirit: the patio, garden, animal pens. Alongside this belief in the home's tutelary spirit, the Aimara people will put a cross and/or image of a Catholic saint on a wall or shelf to also guarantee the home.

5. Illa

The *illa* or *mama illa* is the protector spirit for cattle and domestic animals, which also helps them to reproduce. The name is probably associated with the Aimara word, *illapa*, meaning lightening. It is associated with the name of the most majestic snowy peaks in the Altiplano, Illimani and Illampu, who are thought to be the creators of rain and lightning. The illas, however, are not exclusively domestic animal spirits; they also cover other things that are important for domestic life, like clothing, agricultural produce, and money.

6. Ajayu

The *ajayu* differs from the previous examples in that it is not considered a deity as such, but a component of each human being at a personal level. The human being can have two or more spirits; the "soul", the "soul body" and the ajayu. The soul is what could be understood as a person's spirit, which separates from the soul body when death approaches. The soul body is laid to rest, but the soul travels away, crosses water and goes to God, returning, according to Aimara belief, every All Saints' Day. The ajayu, which means 'spirit as our vital strength', joins the soul when a person dies. The ajayu is not so much part of the body; it is more like a shadow. It can be lost if the person gets a fright, or it may walk some distance away from the person. When its person is sleeping, it goes elsewhere and talks to other people's ajayus or is visited by them.[18]

Evil Spirits

These spirits' work is to harm human beings although some are ambivalent and can do good or evil, as is the case with the *tio* or *tios*, which must be kept happy. These spirits do not have a defined form or condition and can appear to people in different appearances or behaviours. They usually do not have their own names, but they have particular places where they live and specific times for going out. They trick people by appearing in a form that is attractive to the person they want to harm. These evil spirits encourage spells and curses, which are cast by sorcerers. Aimara men and woman are constantly alert to make sure they are not captured by any of those powers, protecting themselves via rituals that are meant to keep the evil spirits at bay. Although it is believed that no spirit is completely evil, all of them are very hungry. If well fed, they will protect and provide using their extraordinary gifts; but, if not, they can cause illness, death, and natural disaster. The more one enters into the Aimara belief system, the blurrier becomes the border between tutelary spirits and evil spirits, and between dangerous and protector spirits, with one apparently being able to turn into the other.

1. Supay or supaya

Supay is translated as the devil and understood to be its synonym. It is the highest-level evil spirit, ruling over all others. It seeks to take over and possess people's souls, moving around in unknown inhospitable places. Before the arrival of the Spanish, the supay was an ambivalent spirit, both good and evil, but it was gradually transformed by the Catholic Church into the devil himself.

2. Saxra

A *saxra* is an evil spirit who obeys the supay. Saxra is not one, but many; they wander about all the space occupied by the Aimara people. They live in dust storms and go out and about at night, causing sickness, and making people lose their souls.

---

18. Spedding, 91–92.

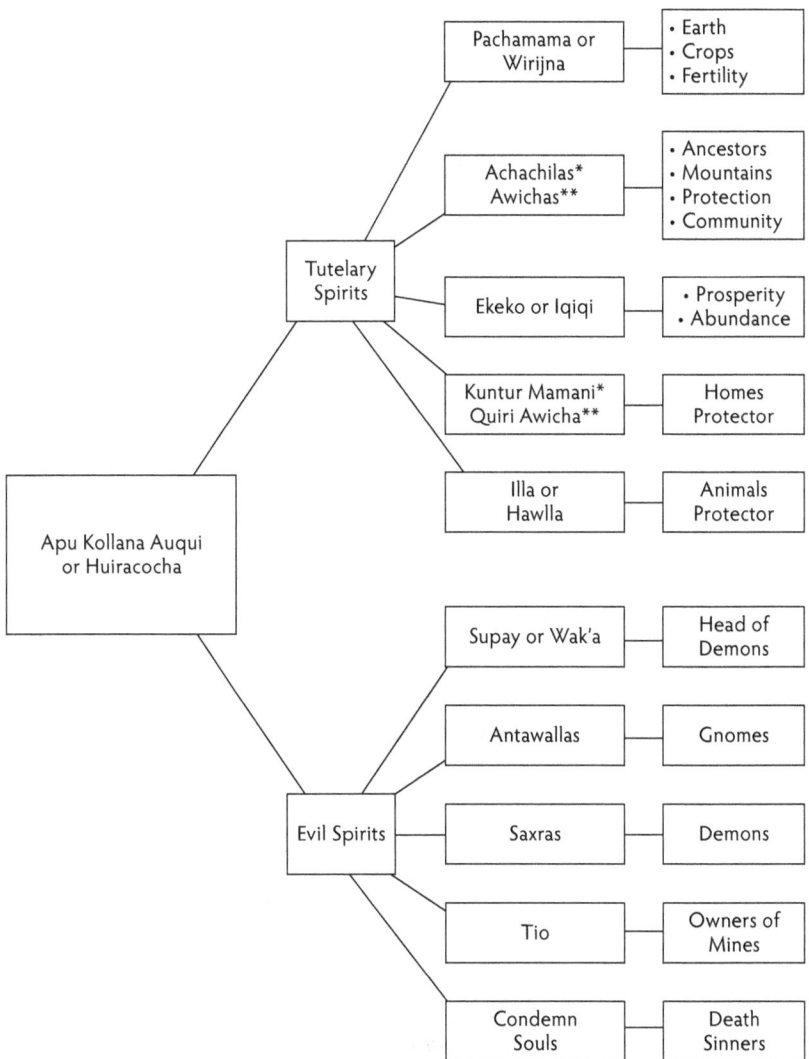

Figure 2: Taxonomy of the Aimaran Pantheon and Its Powers, following the construction of Bouysse-Cassagne, Therese.

3. Antawalla

Antawalla are small spirits who look like human dwarfs and sometimes carry a candle or lit wick in their hands. They like to wander around damp places on dark nights. If people see one, they can become sick or insane, or die.

4. Tio

This is the evil spirit who is believed to own the mines and their mineral resources. Although he can be likened to Satan, he can also be benevolent if he receives the right number and type of offerings. Aimaran miners believe that, by making a pact with the tio, they will receive protection, find lots of minerals, and become rich. The tio is said to appear in dreams or to miners working underground.

5. Condemned souls

These are the spirits of men and women who have sinned, lost their faith in God, and died unrepentant. After death, they wander around the world. They are the souls of people who have come out of their graves because they lived bad lives.

Rituals and Tables

Aimara rituals can be divided into three categories: those that fall into the Catholic calendar and are closely linked to Andean agricultural work, rites of passage, and those related to offering tables. All three depend on and complement each other. In the cycle of rituals based on the Catholic calendar, the dates that coincide with the pre-Catholic indigenous calendar have become more important. The high point is in November, known in Aimara as the *aya marca quilla*, that is, the "month of the people of the dead." This was the month for remembering the dead, so it was easy to combine with the Catholic All Saints' Day, also in November.

The Aimara ritual calendar starts in August to coincide with the end of the farming year and the beginning of the new one:

- August – sowing rituals with the family and on the hillside
- 2 August – Day of the Indian
- 6 August – Independence Day
- 15 August – Assumption of the Virgin
- 8 September – Birth of the Virgin
- 14 September – Lord of Exultation
- 1 November – All Saints' Day, start of rainy season
- 2 November – Day of the Dead
- 25 December – Christmas – the baby Jesus blesses children, the harvest, and cattle
- 1 January – New Year

- 2 February – Celebration of the Virgin of Copacabana
- February/March – Catholic Carnival
- April/May – Lent
- May/Pentecost – the *mamata* (mother seed), harvest thanksgiving
- 21 June – Winter Solstice
- 24 June – Saint John's Day
- 29 June – Saint Peter's and Saint Paul's Day
- 16 July – Virgin of Carmen's Day
- 25 July – Start of Independence Day celebrations
- 31 July – Start of *ch'allas* (offerings) to the Pachamama

Although this is a list of the most common annual rituals, every region adapts and modifies each one to reflect particular beliefs and practices. It would be virtually impossible to try to mention each Aimara ritual since, in addition to the Christianized festivals, there are also numerous ancestral rituals still celebrated by the Aimaras living in the rural and urban areas. The rituals involve simple or multiple offerings. The simple and most common offering is the ch'alla, which is a libation to the Pachamama. Before drinking some form of alcohol, people will tip a small amount out of their glass onto the ground as an offering for Mother Earth. One thing is certain, Aimara rituals have indigenized Catholic Christianity, but the opposite has not occurred. At the arrival of the first missionaries jointly with the conquerors, slaves' conversion was superfluous. In practical ritualistic terms, syncretism did occur but not meaningfully, even though Andean rituals include Christian elements like the crucifix, bells, pictures of saints, candles, and prayers like the Ave Maria and Lord's Prayer.

Traditional animistic customs are seen most clearly in rituals. Despite persistent inequalities between Aimara peasants and Aimara mestizo town residents, both groups share a marked ritualistic behaviour. Ch'alla[19], *q'uwa*[20] and *sahumerio*[21] are the most important and most commonly practised Aimara rituals. They are popular religious expressions in La Paz and throughout Bolivia, especially in terms of honouring Pachamama.

---

19. *Ch'alla*, libation with alcoholic drinks to different divinities especially Pachamama. It consists of pouring a portion of alcoholic drink from one's glass onto the ground before downing the rest. Albó, *Raices de America*, 589.

20. *Q'uwa* This is a wild mint often used in rituals. The aromatic plant is burnt in the offering. *Q'uacha* is an offering with *q'uwa*. Albó, 602.

21. *Sahumerio* The smoke from the burnt wild aromatic plant is passed over the offerings.

Rites of Passage

Birth
The Aimara belief is that one is born into life as the son of the achachila, because the new baby belongs to the ancestors. During the delivery, the mother receives special attention and food to protect her from the forces of nature. Birth is considered a sacred, but dangerous, moment and therefore special prayers and offerings are made. Birth is linked to ancestral forces and the sacred forces of nature; the Aimara appeal to these for shelter and protection and try to appease them.

Baptism
The Aimaras believe that the *wawa* or baby becomes a member of the Christian social world at baptism. Godparents are chosen to serve as role models for the child and a long-lasting reciprocal relationship is forged between the baby's family and the godparents. The parents and the godparents take the wawa to the church, where the baptism ceremony also serves to name the child. This ritual is also believed to cover or protect the child from the dark side of the ancestors or the achachilas.

Rutucha
The next important step in a child's life is the *rutucha* or first haircut. Again, godparents of some influence in society are chosen, although they may be the same as the ones who serve as baptism godparents. They give the child new clothes, which he or she will wear after the haircut. Friends and family gather to eat together, the godparents cut off the first lock of hair, wrap some money around it, and place it on a plate amidst toasts and jokes. The money is to help the child survive in the real world and, therefore, this ritual represents the child entering the economic life of the family and community.

Fifteenth Birthday
One initiation rite into adult life that has been adopted by many Aimara in the urban area is the fifteenth birthday for young women. Parents, relatives, and godparents join together to hold a party, with dancing and drinking, where the new fifteen-year-old is presented as a woman. This is a very common practice among the middle and upper Bolivian classes.

Military Service
Young men are introduced to adult life via a party held at eighteen years of age when they finish their year of military service. This celebration is particularly

common among the economically poorer classes. The tough life in the army – separated from the family and women – with its discipline, physical exercise, and patriotism, are seen to prepare the men for marriage. At the party, the men receive household gifts and people pin money to their jacket lapel – all of which is to help them set up home.

Completing Secondary School
Finishing secondary school is considered an important step towards assuming the economic responsibilities of an adult. After a graduation ceremony at school, the school leavers hold a big party with family and friends, with lots of food, drink, and dancing. Again, godparents are named; they usually pay something towards the party and give the boy or girl a special gift.

Marriage
In Aimara tradition, a couple will start living together for a period known as "mutual service" or *sirwiñaku*. On forming their home, the Aimara becomes a *jaqi*, which means 'person'. It is like being born again to assume the responsibilities of reciprocity with their new family, the community and society. The opposite would be a *q'ara* or "naked". The sacred incorporation into the social world that started at birth reaches its culmination with marriage. After marriage, the person reaches the maturity to behave with responsibility and solidarity.

Death
Death entails several complex ceremonies over quite a long period of time. First comes the wake, then the burial, the washing of the deceased person's clothes, the nine-day mass, the one-year mass, and the All Saints' Day masses and special offering tables which are observed for three years after the loved one's death. People wear black for a year after the death and are not supposed to do certain things, like dance or have fun. The belief is that after death comes eternal rest or eternal punishment and the deceased's path towards God's judgement is full of thorns. The different masses and ceremonies are believed to help the deceased person on his road cross a river to come before God who will judge him for his actions while alive. If he was good, he will be accepted into paradise; but, if not, he will be sent back to earth to wander around as a condemned soul until he pays for his wrongs and is accepted in heaven.

Tables

Rituals are almost always accompanied by tables of offerings, which may be simple or involve several different components. The use of aromatic smoke, usually incense, which is wafted around the person or object to be blessed, and a table laden with objects that symbolize food for the spirit are the most common elements of Aimara offerings. People believe these tables are absolutely vital. One curious aspect is that the word *misa*, which means mass in Spanish, is confused with *mesa*, or table, by Aimaras who have difficulty pronouncing the letter "e" and, as a result, the ritual misa in the Catholic Church involves preparing a mesa outside the church. Here it can be observed that the Catholic priest and the Aimara priest are seen to be equally valid religious agents.

The Aimara tables are for the benefactor or malign spirits who need a table because they are always hungry. The belief is that, after eating, the spirits are satisfied and want to bless the person offering the food. If, on the other hand, the food offerings are meagre, then the spirits will become angry. Since spirits eat food not eaten by humans, several of the components on the table are inedible. You can buy already prepared tables in Bolivian markets, but the ritual requires that, during the ceremony, each element be placed on the table in a certain order, duly accompanied by prayers and other activities.

Nowadays, these tables are prepared on coloured paper, with the colour indicating the table's purpose. White paper, for example, is for blessings, green for crops and harvest, and black for curses. Other items are placed on the paper, like small glasses, shells, corn husks, a piece of alpaca or sheep wool weaving, and sprigs of aromatic plants. More elements are added depending on the purpose of the table and the region. The black and white paper tables are burnt, and the green ones are buried. Other common items are called *pasterios* or mysteries; these are hard square plaques made of sugar, stamped with figures of the virgin, a horse rider, toad, star, skull, etc. The designs used on the mysteries are becoming increasingly more complex. There are now some showing people withdrawing money from the bank, starting military service, and sitting at their stall in the market. The figure of the toad is always present, representing the Pachamama, and the figure of the rider, who represents the *tata* or James the Apostle. Along with the pasterios, the table is laid with sweets, vegetables, flowers, llama grease, and coca leaves placed to form different shapes, depending on the purpose of the table.

The meaning of the table depends on the form in which the elements are ordered in the ritual. The sequence for laying each item down and the place where they are put have symbolic significance; it is usually the yatiri or master who places the items on the table although others may be invited to participate.

In every ritual, the chewing of coca leaves is part of the sequence of events as is the spraying of the table with alcohol, known as the *ch'allado*. The belief is that the spirits are fond of alcohol and that the table needs to be burnt or buried because the spirits are perpetually hungry.

Religious Specialists

The most popular and widely accepted Aimara religious agent is the yatiri. It is the yatiri who leads most of the traditional rituals having been trained in their meaning and preparation. The yatiri knows when, how, and where each ritual should be held. Yatiris vary according to function, and each one is recognized and respected for the work each does. A yatiri is considered an authority in the community, gives continuity to religious tradition, and is set apart from the common people. Hence, yatiri is the common name given to the wise person, healer, soothsayer, and ritualist. Each yatiri operates within a predetermined tradition but can adapt each ritual to his or her own personal taste and specific client's requirements.

Yatiris are self-educated; they do not have shared manuals to guide their activities. Someone becomes a yatiri thanks to some supernatural, spiritual experience to which no-one but themselves has been witnesses, for example, one irrefutable requirement is to have survived being struck by a bolt of lightning. Before being able to perform the rituals and offerings alone, a would-be yatiri must work as an assistant alongside a recognized yatiri. Yatiris offer rituals for all kinds of situations: illnesses, plagues, to make it rain or stop raining, to prosper economically, to find a partner, to end your spouse's unfaithfulness, to find a thief and the objects stolen, to interpret dreams, tell the future, call back an ajayu or soul that has been misplaced, and to give advice. Different means are used to perform these tasks, but one of the most common is by "reading" coca leaves.

Ch'amakani

A *ch'amakani* is a soothsayer or healer who has the power to make the spirits talk and answer questions, something the yatiris cannot do. The spirits who a ch'amakani forces to speak only do so in complete darkness at a session held a night, because they cannot be seen by anyone. Both men and women can be ch'amakanis and yatiris and, although historically men have been more common, the number of women is growing. If these soothsayers or healers are not paid for their services, their work will not have an effect; the person who pays most gets the best, longest-lasting result for his or her money.

Layqa

The witch or wizard, sorcerer or sorceress, who casts spells or curses is called a *layqa*. The name varies depending on what they do; they usually operate in secret because they are not considered to be legal. Sorcery ceremonies aimed at cursing or harming someone use a perhaps surprising number of Catholic symbols – candles are lit, Ave Maria and Lord's Prayers are recited, Saint James is addressed, and crucifixes, bells and rosaries are used – as in a Catholic mass.

Kharisiri or *Kharikhari*

These are mythical personages, dangerous humans, traditionally conceived as Catholic priests but recently regarded as a man or woman who roams about isolated areas, repeating prayers, and having supernatural powers to make people fall asleep so the kharisiri can steal fat from their waists and sell it. The victim awakes without knowing what has happened but afterwards can become ill with fever, pain, and vomiting. The victim also can die if not cured in time. Increasingly it is believed that the *kharisiris* do not really exist; the sicknesses express fears regarding the unknown and journeying alone.

Conclusion

The universal search for God experienced by people everywhere in every era has a particular form of expression among the Aimara peoples in the Andean region. The complex Aimara belief system has not been taken into consideration in the Christianization of the Aimara people, either in the past or today. The Incas and the Spanish, just like the modern Neo-Pentecostals, thought that the Aimaras were not religious, that their spirituality was not valuable to them, or that their belief system would simply disappear as if by magic. The people responsible for Christian mission have failed to assign any importance to the active, vital elements of indigenous spirituality. In many cases, they have elected to see the Aimara's religiosity wholly as being "of the devil", denying any manifestation of divine common grace shown to people everywhere. The abstract parts and practices of a belief system that has existed for centuries have been ignored or discredited, resulting in the formation of a foreign, alienated church, without deep roots in this land or a truly Bolivian identity.

The Aimara people's search for God has been performed with a mixture of providential and fatalistic aspects. Guaygua and Castillo categorically affirm that the Neo-Pentecostals do not believe that the dead play any part in daily life.[22] This is not the case of PoGC members. Members of that church still participate not only in death rituals, but also in other ceremonies that involve other deities and Aimaran religious specialists. It seems that the Aimara's religious worldview is still very much alive for PoGC members, just as that particular form of Neo-Pentecostalism is vibrant in the urban Aimaran religiosity of the city of La Paz.

It could be that Catholic priests, evangelical pastors, and yatiris, each with their own interests and approaches, want to conserve their respective traditions, but the ordinary people who follow each of these three religious expressions appear not to share that concern. Their spirituality is more pragmatic, which facilitates the persistence of syncretism. They are, therefore, the main religious subjects of this research. The question I am asking is, "Are Aimara Neo-Pentecostals simply and creatively materializing the condensation of native cultural elements?"

---

22. Guaygua and Castillo, *Identidades y religion*, 109.

3

Bolivian Neo-Pentecostalism: Historical Context

Early Bolivian Christian History
Aimaras in Pre-Colonial and Colonial Times

The precise origin of the Aimara is unknown. However, the deepest, most antique part of Bolivian history is found in the development of Aimaran kingdoms in the central part of the Andean mountains from the end of the twelfth century to the arrival of the Spanish in the sixteenth century.[1] From the middle of the fifteenth century until the arrival of the Spanish, a period of about 100 years, the Aimaras lived under the political and economic control of the Incas. Then came almost 300 years in which the Spanish invaded the Aimaras' territory and life, ruling over them, and implementing an unsuccessful strategy of genocide.

Under the Inca Empire, the Aimaras were not forced to adopt another culture, customs, or language other than their own. The Incas allowed them to preserve their identity and beliefs. There was never one king or Aimaran *cacique* (tribal leader) that dominated all the Aimara kingdoms, rather, local leaders led each group. Just like other existing ethnic groups, the Aimara formed a strong sense of unity in the Altiplano. The philosophical, anthropological, historical, and linguistic studies performed to date by a variety of researchers provide evidence of this reality.

The Inca's dominion over the Andean region lasted until 1537 when the Spanish defeated Atahuallpa, the last Inca. The arrival of the Europeans began a resistance, that although generally passive and secret, was sometimes violent and organized. Several uprisings occurred during the colonial period: the most

---

1. Klein, Bolivia: the evolution of a multi-ethnic society, 15

important rebellion was led by the Aimaran leader, Tupac Katari, from 1780 until 1783 and involved the whole Aimaran territory.

From their arrival in 1492, the Spanish conquerors used Christianity to serve the political interests of the Spanish Empire. They disguised their ambition to possess the immense wealth owned by the indigenous people with exalted, mystic Roman Catholic motivations.[2] In that same year, 1492, the Spanish finally won an 800-year battle against their Islamic enemies. This led to Spain and all of its conquered lands being declared exclusively for Christ and for Christians. This tremendous coincidence fired the fervour of Spanish Christianity and set the conquistadors in motion. Both the soldiers and the priests who accompanied them, with very few exceptions, brought a message that was strongly religious, but completely void of ethical content. A Catholic liturgy adapted to indigenous customs and a superficial catechism made it easy for indigenous groups to keep hold of their traditional spiritual beliefs while nominally embracing Christianity.

The invaders used the sword and the cross as their weapons to subdue the people when they pursued and fought the natives. They brought with them an exogenous cultural system from foreign lands however this system, represented by very different political, economic, religious, and social realities, could not displace the strong Aimaran identity and related lifestyles.

During the colonialist period the wide variety of ethnic groups previously controlled by the Incas were treated as people without their own identity, were not respected, and were dismissively called "Indians". The Spanish reduced all indigenous people to a low, subordinate level considering them all to be culturally and economically the same. Xavier Albó made a revealing analysis, classifying the fixations practised by the Spaniards with the natives into three parts – social, geographical and linguistic.[3] For the Aimara, who comprised several ancient ethnic groups with one common language, these colonialist fixations paradoxically deepened their mutual identification and consolidation as a unique people and culture.

The situation of the Aimaras under the Spanish did not change substantially with independence. The geographical and political division that took place with the independence of Bolivia on 6 August 1825 divided the Aimaras into three different nationalities – Chilean, Peruvian, and Bolivian. With the arrival of the Republic, the Aimara people simply changed oppressor, for oppression

---

2. Mackay, *El Otro Cristo Español*, 50–55.
3. Albó, *Raices de America*, 26.

continued though now led by the Creole[4] authorities who imposed a feudal private property system.[5] Aimaras previously did not conceive land as a matter of private property, their ownership was communal or more than that; their perception was that they belonged to Mother Earth, not the opposite. The Aimara's means of survival was their isolation and non-participation in the national way of life. They moved away from the centres of political and economic power to survive and to continue cultivating their own culture in the remote, rural, Altiplano land. Nowadays, Aimaras' experience that is authentic and distinctive maintains and develops its identity. In this process of continuous reconstruction the ethnic tradition has more weight than the Westernized Hispanic-Creole tradition.

Before the Spanish invasion Aimara kingdoms were not united. Their more definitive settling in the wide Altiplano space probably took place around 1200 BC when the Tiahuanaco culture was in decline. Xavier Albó in the introductory chapter of the monumental compilation on the Aimara world when referring to her historical roots says:

> The diverse ethnic groups settled in the region faced all of them with the need to find similar solutions to one common challenge: The Andes great mountainous mass, with their altitudes and depths in continuous alternation, their annual combination of drought and humidity, their double natural barrier with the sea to a side and the tropical forest to the other one....... Completely part of the shared cultural solution implies strong exchanges and transfers from one to another part of this Andean universe. This permanent interaction also facilitated to emerge an "Andean culture" with many common features, without destroying the peculiarities of many clearly identified ethnic groups and differed as such. Inside that Andean unity-differentiation, what the Aymara will be?[6]

Despite several hypotheses, more than five centuries after the Spanish invasion the pre-Columbian cultures, times, and spaces are still an enigma that invites us to commit to serious research about the importance and dignity of the Andean natives. Murra (1988:51–73), however, has demonstrated that an Aimaran kingdom (called Lupaca before the arrival of the Incas) existed

---

4. In the Bolivian case, Creole was the Spanish descendant born and settled in the geographical limits of the country.

5. Llanque, *La cultura Aymara*, 35.

6. Albó, *Racies de America*, 23–24.

in communities in the Andean mountain range west of Lake Titicaca, at an altitude above 12,000 feet or 4,000 metres.[7] The walls of large settlements of up to sixty hectares have been discovered with "crop platforms, corrals for camelids, dwellings and funeral 'chullpa.'"[8] Murra concludes that extensive archaeological investigation is still required, but pre-Incan remains found above 4000 metres in this region almost certainly belong to the indigenous Lupaca.

Aimara Encounter with Spanish Catholicism

> When I walked among the ruins of their old castles, their solemn temples, their royal roads, their aqueducts that have supported the hand of time, and the beating of the elements, I asked myself, where are those powerful kings that ordered the ingenious artists that erected these magnificent works; animals of natural size made of gold and silver; where are their astronomical observatories; where are their wise and equal laws, their paternal government, their institutions of charity and their religion? The entire world responds, they have perished at the hands of violence and superstition![9]

The Spanish rule over the Aimaras had been consolidated by 1538, just six years after their initial arrival. The Aimara leaders were threatened by the conquerors who asked the natives to hand over their lands and join either the well-organized Spanish military or religious missionary forces.

On first arriving, the conquerors thought they had arrived in India, but later named the continent "America". With an arrogant Renaissance mind that defended and justified slavery, they saw the Aimara as wild, lawless, closer to animals than human beings, lacking culture, history, and religion. They considered the indigenous people inferior, especially in the spiritual realm, calling them pagans and instruments of Satan. This mentality of denying the other and affirming themselves as superior justified subduing the natives and led to a historical ethnic genocide.

The aim of the Spanish was to reduce the Aimaran population by splitting them up into small groups and forcing them into hard labour in the Potosí mines; the obligatory *mita* (a form of public service during the Incan Empire)

---

7. Murra, "*El aymara libre de hoy,*" 51-73.
8. Murra, 55.
9. Cited in Bowman, *Vicente Pazos Kanki*, 32.

was idealized and implemented by Viceroy Francisco de Toledo (1515–1581).[10] Together with pro-slavery exploitation, the objective of the Spanish was to extirpate indigenous religious beliefs and ignorance in the matter of salvation and teach them the Catholic faith.

Marzal says that the colonizers were legally commissioned as missionaries by the Spanish crown under the rules of the Patronato Regio.[11] The Spanish king first persuaded Pope Alejandro VI in 1493, and then Pope Julio II in 1507, to authorise a treaty called Patronato Regio, which consisted of granting missionary status to the Spanish colonising efforts. This implied that the bishops and priests were not only appointed by Spanish King Felipe IV but also paid by him rather than by the Pope in Rome.

In the following honest and painful testimony, Marzal, a Catholic priest, gives some insight into the character of the Patronato:

> In the early evangelism, there was a first ethnocide stage promoted by the conquerors to rationalize their preys, although performed without much subjective sincerity, like the missionaries, because of their theological presuppositions. This ethnocide evangelism occurred more in Mexico and Peru because of the wealth of its temples and the complexity of its religions… [12]

This quotation helps us to understand that what was called "evangelism" did not bring "good news"; indeed, it was very bad news for the natives. The regime of Patronato was an accomplice of the ethnocide because it disguised the evil alliances formed between priests and chief magistrates against Andean Aimaras and Quechuas.

> Then in a relatively brief period, less than one century, the image of the Christian god hid that of the Sun, which had replaced already that of Viracocha in previous times, successor in turn of Tunupa.[13]

Spanish theology basically taught that the Spaniards' religion was the true one and that of the Indians was diabolical. According to José de Acosta, the theologian that presented the very influential De procuranda indorum salute in the III Council of Lima (1588), Indian religions were diabolical and any similarity with the Catholic religion was a "parody of the devil."[14]

---

10. Mesa Gisbert et al, *Historia de Bolivia*, 97–104.
11. Marzal, *Tierra encantada*, 266.
12. Marzal, 268.
13. Bouysse-Cassagne, *La Identidad Aymara*, 217.
14. Marzal, *Tierra encantada*, 269.

What Indians Are These?

The abuses practised by the Spanish gave rise to indigenous rebellions. The pioneer Aimaran movement for independence was led by Tomas Katari in the north of Potosí in 1781 and spread as far as the capital of the viceroyalty of La Plata, Buenos Aires. This Aimara rebellion against the unjust treatment received from the Spanish did not prosper because of tactical errors and disloyalty. The more representative and genuine Aimaran rebellion was led by Tupac Katari (Julian Apaza 1750–1781)) and was based on the horizontal leadership of the Aimaras. Decisions were made in consultation with the Council of Mallkus. The Aimaras did not accept the Amaru's Quechua leadership because they were not willing to accept the Quechuas' vertical impositions.[15] This is another indication that the Aimara's decision-making processes were and are horizontal, not vertical. At family and communal levels, decision-making about social, religious, economic, and political matters was and is performed collectively.

The official history written by Catholic elitist authors has ignored the Amaru's and the Katari's vision regarding the identity and destiny the Andean natives wanted to give to the continent. Thirty years after the defeat of Tupac Amaru and Katari, the Aimaras viewed the wars for independence with distrust. Neither the Quechua nor the Aimara accepted the independence offered by the Creoles as a valid or positive alternative for them.

Aimaras in Republican Times

The Republican era simply meant a change of masters, with the Creoles and some Roman Catholic mestizos replacing the Spanish. Political power was granted to authorities that were Creole and landowners who lived near the towns. The indigenous people continued to be enslaved and their lands plundered; all kinds of laws were made to legitimize these acts. However, the Aimara never considered themselves as having been conquered. According to Cardenas they see themselves as "oppressed but not conquered."[16] Over the years, Aimara uprisings broke out to complain about the abuses practised by governments and landowners.

During the Chaco war (1932–35), the Aimara and Quechua fought side-by-side in battle and, as never before, they created a sense of being the foundation of the Bolivian people. During that war, the trade union movement appeared, formed by workers, craftsmen, and miners of Aimara and Quechua origin.

---

15. Llanque, *La cultura Aymara*, 33.
16. Cardenas, "La lucha de un pueblo," 495.

These trade unions, organized in a native manner, sought greater justice, and worked for reforms to benefit the Aimara and Quechua people. (The Quechuas were the first to organize and establish their own schools; this did not happen in Aimara regions, because the landowners were stronger and more jealous.) This trade union movement ended in the bloody revolution of 1952 after achieving the approval of laws that abolished slavery in all its forms. In 1945, it was referred to in Spanish as *pongueaje* and *mita* in a national Congress meeting called by President Gualberto Villarroel (1908–46). After the elections in 1951 were won by the Revolutionary Nacionalistis Movement (RNM) (a populist party), agrarian reform was approved. The landowners were sent out of their alleged lands and the natives occupied it.

Even with its limitations, this period marked the emergence of an Aimaran movement willing to fight for its rights despite disadvantageous conditions. Since that time, the movement has become increasingly strong in political, professional, linguistic, and cultural terms.

Aimaran Evangelicals and Pentecostalism
The Arrival of the Protestant Missionaries

Research shows the first mention of Protestants in Bolivian territory occurred during the war that won independence from the Spanish in August 1825. Arias affirms that the first Protestants to step on Bolivian land were possibly British members of the army (led by the liberator Simón Bolivar) that freed Alto Peru.[17] There is no evidence that these European army officers attempted to proselytize the Bolivia Aimaras or anyone else in Bolivia.

However, it is possible that the Aimaras came into contact with Protestant Christians even before the republican era. Little is known with certainty but some Europeans from Protestant countries like Germany and Ireland came to work in mining, agriculture, and industry before independence with Spanish approval and authorization.[18] These prosperous immigrants, mostly from a Protestant background, could not have carried out their managerial projects without using indigenous labour – which leads us to wonder about

---

17. Dussel et al, *Historia General de la Inglesia en America Latina*, 260. The Andean Amazonian territory called Alto Peru, was liberation in 1825, named Bolivar Republic in remembrance of the liberator. See Mesa Gisbert et al, *Historia de Bolivia*, 321. A year later the name was changed to Bolivia.

18. Crespo, *Alemanes en Bolivia*.

the exchange between the European immigrants' religion and Aimaran and Quechuan beliefs before the nineteenth century.

There is, however, considerable evidence about the first Protestant who made a significant contribution to education and Bible distribution and translation in Latin America – the Scotsman James Thomson (1788–1854). He was an official collaborator in the implementation of Lancastrian[19] educational systems in the recently founded republics of Argentina, Chile, Peru, and Venezuela.[20] He was also a representative of the British Bible Society and, as such, a promoter of Bible translation and reading in native languages. It is believed that having interviewed the liberator Simón Bolivar before the Battle of Junin, he decided to visit Bolivia.

Pazos Kanki was a well-known Aimaran thinker and writer who was born in 1779 near Sorata in the community of Santa Maria of Ananea and died in Buenos Aires in 1852. He witnessed indigenous revolutions against the Spanish Empire and revolutionary independence movements. He had a gift for languages and spoke fluent Latin and some indigenous languages. In 1805, he was ordained as a Catholic priest in Chuquisaca, the most famous intellectual centre in South America, which compared, at that time, with Oxford University in England. His liberal ideas and thirst for justice made him part of the independence movement in La Paz in 1808–09. Fearing for his life, Pazos Kanki moved to Buenos Aires in 1810 where he left the priesthood to work in journalism.[21] He became very well known in Buenos Aires under the name Vicente Pasos Silva and was an outstanding journalist, shaping public opinion in Buenos Aires via the columns that he wrote as director of the newspapers *La Gazeta* and *El Censor*.[22]

Because of his active participation in political movements in favour of freedom and independence, Pasos Kanki was pursued, arrested, and exiled. When living as a political exile in London in 1826, he met James Thomson while travelling on public transport, and a fruitful friendship developed.[23] Thomson persuaded Pazos Kanki, on behalf of the British and Foreign Bible Society, to translate the Bible into the Aimara language at that time spoken

---

19. This was a very influential educational system in the western World in the first half of the nineteenth century. It was created by the Anglican Pastor, Andrew Bell, in 1797 but amplified by Joseph Lancaster. This system consisted of one teacher teaching a group of students or a whole school using few materials; the Bible was used as a textbook.

20. Canclini, *Diego Thomson*, 21–24.

21. Bowman, *Vicente Pazos Kanki*, 27–42.

22. Dussel et al, *Historia General de la Iglesia en America Latina*, 260.

23. Canclini, *Diego Thomson*, 89.

by one million natives living around the shores of Lake Titicaca. Luke's gospel was translated first directly from the Vulgate; the first edition of this important work was published in London in 1829. The translation work carried out by this Aimaran intellectual served as a fundamental basis for the Aimara version of the Bible now published and distributed by the Bolivian Bible Society. Mariscal Andrés de Santa Cruz appointed Pasos Kanki Consul General for Bolivia in England in 1836.[24]

The first attempt by missionaries to establish a permanent Protestant work in Bolivia was unsuccessful. In 1846, an officer from the British Royal Army, Captain Allen F. Gardiner (1794–1851), became the first Anglican missionary in Latin America.[25] He wanted to begin a mission in Potosí. President Ballivian authorized him to work among non-Catholic indigenous people in northern Potosí, teaching them the Protestant faith and improving their living conditions. When Gardiner returned to Bolivia in 1848, the new Bolivian president José Miguel de Velasco refused to honour any agreements his predecessor had made with the English missionary. Gardiner was forced to leave Bolivia and went to Patagonia, where he died of starvation in 1851 together with five other missionaries. In doing so, he became the martyr's seed for Anglican missionary work, not just with indigenous people, but throughout Latin America under the South American Missionary Society (SAMS).

One Century of Consolidation

Towards the middle of the nineteenth century Protestant missions were in every South American country, except Bolivia and Ecuador. While Brazil already had 116 Protestant missionaries and Argentina had 112, in Bolivia there were none. The Baptist and the Brethren Churches arrived at the end of this century. William Payne, from the Irish Brethren Church, was the first to arrive for an exploratory trip in 1895. He first visited the capital, Sucre, where a jealous Catholic archbishop took away his last box of Protestant Bibles. In 1896, Archibald Reekie, a Canadian Baptist, paid a short visit to La Paz and then returned to Bolivia in 1898, settling in Oruro.

Another important landmark in the history of Protestantism in Bolivia was the small-scale agrarian reformation in an Aimara community called Huatajata on Lake Titicaca. Between 1936–41 the Baptists gave property title deeds to native Aimara (including non-Protestants), twelve years before the government

---

24. Bowman, *Vicente Pazos Kanki*, 218.
25. Deiros, *Historia del Cristianismo*, 669–70.

adopted the agrarian reform for the whole country. The Baptists bought the Huatajata farm, together with its 48 families and 275 servants, with funds donated by the Italian North American, Antonio Chirioto. They then donated the land, making the families the legal owners at a time when the indigenous Aimara lived as slaves.[26] People who witnessed this event still comment that Víctor Paz Estensoro and Hernan Siles Suazo, who were the leaders of the 1952 Revolution, presidents of the country, and the main idealists of the agrarian reformation at national level, received inspiration from the Baptist Protestants' example in Huatajata.

Former Vice President Víctor Hugo Cardenas (in office 1993–97) was the first Aimara to occupy such a high position in government.[27] He and his wife were born in Huatajata and were part of the Baptist Church tradition that valued the Aimaran context of working in agriculture, education, and health.[28]

The Methodists followed the Brethren's and Baptist's missionary efforts. The Evangelical Indian Mission, which promoted the translation of the New Testament into Quechua[29] and founded a denomination called the UCE (Evangelical Christian Union), came next. The Adventists were the last to arrive in this first missionary period.

The records of pioneer churches which contain lists of the first converts to be baptized, pictures of regional and national events, testimonies, reports, etc., show the massive participation of Aimaras in the La Paz, Oruro, and Potosí churches. The writings of Goytia and Zúñiga highlight the work carried out by solitary foreign missionaries, indicating that the great conquest of evangelical Christian work in Bolivia is attributable mainly to these foreigners.[30] However, their own books show the massive, active work of Bolivians, particularly indigenous believers.

In Bolivia, the Bible written in native languages has been, and continues to be, a useful tool for teaching excluded sectors of the population to read and write, raising their awareness of Christianity. Indeed, it has not been the Scripture or the gospel itself that has represented the biggest obstacle to indigenous people and their relationship with evangelical Christianity, but the cultural "robe" imported by the missionaries. The missionaries, either

---

26. Nacho, "Historia Bautista," 89.

27. Mesa Gisbert, *Historia de Bolivia*, 703.

28. Comisión Conferencia Misioneros Bautistas en Bolivia, *El cincuentenario de la Mision Bautista Canadiense*, 15

29. Hudspith, *Ripening Fruit*, 48.

30. Goytia, *Principios Evangelica en Bolivia*; Zúñiga, *La gran conquista*.

consciously or unconsciously, injected ideological and cultural implants from the West into their projects by using Spanish rather than Aimara or Quechua. This influence was also seen in church building styles, liturgy, clothing, and musical instruments; these reflected an imported way of life rather than a respect for indigenous customs and traditions.

Traditional Pentecostals

The progress made by the Protestant church during its first fifty years of existence was slow and somewhat superficial. Assemblies of God missionaries arrived in 1946 to introduce their version of Pentecostalism, which had first been sown in South America in Valparaiso in Chile and São Paulo in Brazil. This form of Protestant Pentecostalism attracted wide sectors of the population in Chile and Brazil at a time when, in Bolivia, the Protestant church was a minority group composed of poor, mainly indigenous congregations.[31] The Assemblies of God, together with two other pioneer Pentecostal denominations (planted by the Free Swedish Mission and Foursquare Gospel Church)[32] attracted more indigenous converts, built many churches, and communicated a plan that was less Western, more grass-roots and democratic; however these efforts still fell far short of reaching the Bolivian indigenous people's heart and soul.[33]

It should be mentioned here that although Dario Lopez concluded that Latin American Pentecostalism attracted the poorest people while Neo-Pentecostalism reaches the middle class,[34] this is not the case in Bolivia where, as in Central America, the Neo-Pentecostal Church is made up of the poor, who are usually indigenous. Members of traditional Pentecostal churches, on the other hand, are both indigenous and educated middle-class. A similar inaccuracy is made by studies of Chilean and Brazilian Pentecostalism at the beginning of the twentieth century which reach a generalized conclusion that the Pentecostal Church opened the doors mostly to the masses.[35] Bolivian Neo-Pentecostals, who are the direct heirs of traditional Pentecostalism, have taken huge steps towards contextualizing the gospel for the Andean indigenous peoples.

---

31. Míguez Bonino, *Protestantismo Latinoamericano*, 57.
32. Riviere, "Bolivia: el Pentecostalismo," 262.
33. Riviere, 259-94.
34. Lopez, *El nuevo rostro*; Lopez, *La fiesta del Espiritu*.
35. Willems, *Followers of the New Faith*; and D'Epinay, *El Refugio de las Masas*.

Historical Background of Neo-Pentecostalism and the PoGC

Throughout its history Pentecostals have based their faith in the New Testament book, the Acts of the Apostles.[36] This book, written by Luke, narrates the history of the early Christian church. However, many present-day theologians would agree that a more appropriate name for the book is the "Acts of the Holy Spirit" as it records the supernatural way in which the Holy Spirit came to over 120 disciples of Jesus Christ in Jerusalem on the day of Pentecost. There was freedom and spontaneity as the gifts of the Holy Spirit were manifested in the speaking of different languages, in prophecy and healing (Acts 2:1–4).

The gifts, or charismata, given by the Holy Spirit were common in the early church. Their presence is recorded mainly in the Book of Acts, although references are found in the New Testament Epistles. Throughout the history of Christianity, its context, forms of worship, and mission have undergone change, but the supernatural phenomena of the Holy Spirit have been repeated at different times.

After the early church period, Montanus led the first movement that wanted to restore the practice of spiritual gifts in the second century. The church father, Tertullian, is perhaps the best known Montanist theologian. Several church fathers, including Tertullian, received the gifts of the Spirit and none affirmed that the gifts of the Spirit were only for a specific historical period. After the official church rejected the Montanists, the Western church began to preach that charismatic gifts had only been given for biblical times. By 1000 AD, the Roman Catholic Church went as far as to affirm that the gifts from the Holy Spirit were manifestations of demons. Eastern Christianity, however, part of the Orthodox Church, continued to believe in the gifts of the Spirit and practised them in their monasteries in the Middle Ages. With the exception of the Anabaptists, the Protestant Reformation of the sixteenth century dismissed spiritual gifts, because leaders like Luther and Calvin believed they were unimportant for their times. The rationalistic argument they used was that miracles were no longer necessary because science was advancing. Later, isolated Protestant charismatic experiences were reported in Germany, France, England, and Scotland.[37]

Contemporary Pentecostalism dates back to the eighteenth century. Its roots are in Moravian pietism and the Wesleyan Holiness Movement. Contemplative devotion of Christ's cross, personal and literal Bible study, and the denial of worldly pleasures were the marks of Moravian missionaries such

---

36. Romeiro, *Decepcionados com a graça*, 21–23.
37. Anderson, *An Introduction to Pentecostalism*, 19–25.

as those who influenced John Wesley's life, leading him to a second conversion in 1738. This was the flame that resulted in the Methodist Revival. Several other charismatic movements in North America and Europe have affected Pentecostalism, although the Wesleyan revival was the most decisive with its emphasis on what was called, the "second blessing", "filling with power", or "baptism of the Holy Spirit."[38]

The Pentecostal movement, as it is known today, has a variety of origins. It cannot be attributed, as has wrongly been done, uniquely to an origin in the United States even though the primary sources of information from elsewhere are partial and limited. Other existing documentation points to several simultaneous revivals in various locations during the nineteenth and twentieth centuries. From its beginnings, Pentecostalism was a movement in different parts of the world, and not just the United States despite the greater influence from there. Although not always recognized, the contribution made by native Pentecostal preachers from Latin America, Asia, and Africa have been just as important to Pentecostalism as those made by western missionaries.[39]

The revival initiated among African Americans in April 1906 by the black pastor, William J. Seymour (1870–1922), in an old building in 312 Azuza Street, Los Angeles, has become legendary in the history of Pentecostalism. Azuza Street is considered the Pentecostal 'Jerusalem' or its "Mecca."[40] However, without taking away from the importance of what happened in Azusa Street, a diverse movement with the magnitude and impact Pentecostalism has had cannot be sustained by legends made in North America or other isolated places. As Everett Wilson said, "Pentecostalism cannot become a possession of any sector neither of certain groups in particular nor had a single origin because there were several beginnings."[41]

Let us look more closely at the origins of Pentecostalism in Latin America, now the most Pentecostal continent in the world with 141 million members (including the Neo-Pentecostal movement).[42] Freston suggests that a more realistic figure is 60 million, of which two thirds are Pentecostals and Neo-Pentecostals.[43] Chile would appear to have been the birthplace of Pentecostalism in Latin America. In the largest Methodist Church of the city of Valparaiso

---

38. Romeiro, *Decepcionados com a graça*, 27–31.
39. Anderson, *An Introduction to Pentecostalism*, 166–70.
40. Anderson, 171; and Nichol, *Pentecostalism*, 34.
41. Wilson, *They crossed the Red Sea, didn't they?* 107.
42. Barret and Johnson, *World Christian Trends*, 2003, 287
43. Freston, "Latin America: The 'Other Christendom,'" 571–94.

the US pastor, Willis C. Hoover (1858–1936), together with his wife, had a Pentecostal experience in 1907. The Hoovers were influenced by a revival led by Pandita Ramabai in an orphanage for young women in Pune, India, that started in 1905. They also heard, through Methodist colleagues, about similar revivals happening in other parts of the world, like Venezuela and Norway. They encouraged the church they led to pray for a revival of the Holy Spirit.

In April 1909, they experienced charismatic manifestations such as speaking in tongues, seeing visions, uncontrollable laughing and crying, and falling to the floor; these were followed by intensive preaching in the streets. The local Methodist leaders, public authorities, and press reacted against the revival. Those who had been baptized with the Holy Spirit were expelled from the Episcopal Methodist Church, which also wanted to send the Hoovers back to the United States for a year as a preventive measure. However, the Chilean church members persuaded the Hoovers to establish a new church, and the Pentecostal Methodist Church was born; today it is the largest Chilean denomination with 300,000 members.[44] A Chilean, Manuel Umana Salinas, started pastoring this church in 1911, becoming its main leader after Willis Hoover. It is important to highlight that this movement was completely autochthonous, having no connection with the North American Pentecostal movement. From the start, it was different to nearly all the current Chilean Pentecostal denominations, having its own particular identity,[45] which Deiros describes in the following way:

> Autochthonous Chilean Pentecostalism was characterized by long pastorates of very popular leaders. Hoover himself led their congregation for more than a quarter of a century. This Pentecostalism was also marked by being the heir of the Methodist Episcopal church inasmuch as it had an authoritarian leadership, wide lay participation, autonomy in managing church affairs, a populist attitude inherited from Catholicism and an extraordinary motivation for the evangelization of the masses.[46]

In Argentina, the story was different. Pentecostalism arose in the immigrant community, where it remained for several years. Millions of immigrants arrived in Argentina in the first part of the twentieth century; most were European, and many were Protestants. In 1909, the Norwegian Berger Johnson, the Canadian

---

44. Anderson, *An Introduction to Pentecostalism*, 64–67.
45. Anderson, 64–67.
46. Deiros, *Historia del Cristianismo*, 752.

Alice Wood, and the US Italian Luigi Francescon were the main pioneers, each working in different parts of Argentina. Later, Swedish missionaries from the Free Swedish Mission founded a work that formed an association with the Assemblies of God Church from the United States.

On comparing Chilean and Argentinean Pentecostalism, Martin shows the social character of both their foundations:

> Whereas Protestantism in Argentina largely reflects cultural traits imported by immigrants from Protestant countries, in Chile Protestantism it is the result of evangelization carried on by Chilean working people among those of their own class. They gathered in the environs of the great cities.[47]

The Pentecostal version of Brazilian Protestantism began with lay missionaries of Italian and Swedish origin from Chicago. Both groups began their ministry in 1910 in already-established Presbyterian and Baptist churches, from which they were subsequently expelled. After some time in Buenos Aires, Luigi Francescon went to São Paulo accompanied by Giacomo Lombardi and Lucia Ore. He first made contact with Presbyterian believers since he had been the founder of the first Presbyterian Church of Chicago. The charismatic experiences that followed were rejected by the Brazilian Presbyterian Church leadership but resulted in the foundation of the Christian Congregation of Brazil. This church initially worked exclusively among Italians but in 1930 opened up to Brazilians, leading to extraordinary growth.

That same year, in the far north of Brazil, Daniel Berg and Gunnar Vingren, both Swedes from a Baptist context in Chicago, were received by a Baptist church in Belem do Para, but they were eventually rejected because of their doctrines and Pentecostal practices. They then left the Baptist church with a small group of Brazilian believers and founded the Mission of Apostolic Faith in 1911. This later became the Assemblies of God, the largest Pentecostal denomination in Brazil, in Latin America, and maybe in the world.[48] Anderson gives us a social ethnic portrait of this church in its beginnings:

> The church considers itself an independent church within the worldwide AG (Assemblies of God) fellowship of churches. Members were recruited initially from the lower strata of society, and Pentecostalism appealed to black, mixed race and Amerindian Brazilians. Mullatos (mixed race African and European) are still

---

47. Martin, *Tongues of Fire*, 76.
48. Romeiro, *Decepcionados com a graça*, 37–39.

the majority in the AG – and there are more black Brazilians in Pentecostal churches than in any other denomination.[49]

Míguez Bonino talked about the beginning of the Pentecostal expression of Latin American Protestantism in response to a critique made by the eminent Peruvian thinker, Mariategui:

> What the Peruvian writer could not guess was that, twenty years before, in a Chilean port, and two years later in the growing city of São Paulo, a Protestantism had began to appear just about the time he wrote that would demolish the barrier which had barred Protestantism access to the popular masses.[50]

From their birth these new churches have marked the Pentecostal version of the evangelical church in Latin America, as already seen in the Chilean, Argentinean, and Brazilian experience. This socio-religious phenomenon has been reproduced and multiplied, sometimes in unexpected ways, but most divisions were caused by Latin chauvinism and nepotism. Other features of early Pentecostalism were: members from the poor majority sectors, exclusivist doctrinal and spiritual fundamentalism, emphasis on the emotional experience, and severe disapproval of any use of the intellect.

The history was similar in Bolivia. Gustav Flood and his wife were missionaries from the Free Swedish Mission who arrived in Santa Cruz in 1922.[51] Perhaps they should be credited with the establishment of Pentecostalism in Bolivia. The Chaco War interrupted their work, but it resumed in the 1950s and churches were established in Villamontes, Cochabamba, and La Paz.

The second group of Pentecostal missionaries was from the Four Square Gospel Church that arrived in Trinidad in 1930 and marked the start of Tom Anderson's ministry. Later on, US missionaries led by Nicodemus Hale began the Assemblies of God in 1946 in Bolivia, spreading to La Paz, Cochabamba, and Santa Cruz. This denomination grew numerically more than any other and exhibited its Pentecostal identity via manifestations of the Holy Spirit, such as speaking in tongues, healing, and meetings with widespread emotional experiences.[52]

---

49. Anderson, *An Introduction to Pentecostalism*, 72.
50. Bonino, *Rostros del Protestantismo latinoamericano*, 57.
51. Anderson, *Spreading Fires*, 199–200.
52. Dussel et al, *Historia General de la Iglesia*, 408.

Julio Cesar Ruibal and the Neo-Pentecostal Revival in Bolivia

The revival that gave rise to Neo-Pentecostalism in Bolivia had no direct relationship with the pioneering classical Pentecostalism. The latter's roots lay with North American and European missionaries. The Neo-Pentecostal movement, however, started almost independently, although some Assemblies of God churches in Cochabamba and La Paz had experienced a spiritual awakening and had been praying for a revival since 1970.[53] When Neo-Pentecostals talk about their history they all pinpoint a single event – the 1972–73 revival led by a young Bolivian called Julio Cesar Ruibal, who was not linked to any Pentecostal or evangelical church.

At the beginning of 1972 Julio Cesar Ruibal was studying medicine in Pasadena, California, United States. He had been a practising Roman Catholic throughout his childhood although his youth was marked by a search for mysticism in oriental religions. In Los Angeles, he was teaching yoga and occultism to a young hippie group when he was invited to the Shrine Auditorium where he witnessed healing miracles and heard the preaching of Kathryn Kuhlman (1907–1976).

Kuhlman was an evangelist influenced by the Latter Rain movement, which was formed in 1948 when several Pentecostal denominations joined together to demand the renewal of classical Pentecostalism. Some consider Kuhlman to be the best-known woman evangelist in the world. She started her ministry at the age of sixteen and suffered some setbacks and criticism, especially when she married a man who divorced his first wife to marry her. Kuhlman knew how to use the media, preaching first on radio and then on television; she became so famous that thousands attended her meetings throughout the United States. Her followers include John Arnott, who started the revival known as the "Toronto Blessing", and Benny Hinn, another famous US evangelist. Kuhlman's ministry emphasized healing, being "slain" in the Spirit, and fervent preaching.[54] She meticulously planned every detail of her services and enjoyed the luxury afforded by clothes, jewels, hotels, and vehicles.[55] As a renowned woman preacher, she promoted women's ministry within Pentecostal and Neo-Pentecostal churches.[56]

---

53. De Calderon, *Porque el Senor asi lo prometio*, ix–x.
54. Wilson, *Kathryn Kuhlman (1907-76)*, 826.
55. Buckingham, *Daughter of destiny: Kathryn Kuhlman*, 247.
56. Anderson, *An Introduction to Pentecostalism*, 274. Some authors link Kuhlman with the start of the New Age movement. See Duncan, Kathryn Kuhlman; Chambers "Kathryn Kuhlman and her spirit guide". Some say Kuhlman laid the foundations for a new movement that brings religions together as part of her personal search for one single world religion. She combines

It was in one of Kuhlman's crowded meetings in California that young Julio Ruibal gave himself to Jesus Christ. At eighteen years of age he made a dramatic turnaround in his life, experienced the Holy Spirit, left occultism, and spoke to his yoga students about Jesus before leaving university. In March 1972, only a few weeks after his conversion, Ruibal and some others were unable to get into a meeting led by Kathryn Kuhlman. So, he stood in front of the closed doors, spoke to the people outside about Jesus Christ, and prayed for the sick who, according to reports, were miraculously healed. He stopped studying medicine and started missionary training, first in Canada and then with a group of charismatic Catholics in the United States before returning to Bolivia.[57]

Julio Cesar Ruibal returned to La Paz in August 1972 at the age of nineteen with a vision of starting a spiritual revival similar to ones that had already taken place in other places in Latin America. Through Ruibal, a movement began in Bolivia that could be called a popular movement of the Holy Spirit because its leaders had no academic qualifications in theology or lengthy spiritual training. The lay people who led this renewal were young Bolivians who had a passionate desire to know the Bible and to make it known to others. Rejected by his family, Ruibal lived with friends; his first followers were relatives, old school childhood friends, and neighbours. The members of a famous and much-feared street gang known as The Marquises were among the first young people converted under Ruibal's ministry.[58] He sought support from the evangelical Lutheran Church, an initiative that was rejected.

During this time, Bolivia was governed by its longest ever right-wing military dictatorship, led by General Hugo Banzer Suarez. The law was not respected nor was the Bolivian political constitution. Universities were closed and political and trade union activity was banned.

The military dictatorship played an important role in the emergence of Neo-Pentecostalism as it was a way of diverting the people's attention away from the government's illegality and corruption. Banzer commanded army guards to protect Ruibal and he was given prime time broadcasts on state-owned radio and television stations. The government also facilitated contacts

---

Christianity, spiritualism, and modern psychology with extreme capitalism. She practiced yoga, shared public communion with Catholics, even meeting privately with Pope Paul VI and always reserved the front row of her meetings for Catholic priests and nuns.

57. De Calderon, *Porque el Senor asi lo promentio*, 3–13.

58. De Calderon, 15.

with regional governors to organize preaching events and even made an Air Force aircraft available for his use.[59]

Accompanied by a group of young followers, Julio Cesar Ruibal held preaching and healing campaigns in the main Bolivian cities of La Paz, Oruro, Cochabamba, and Santa Cruz. Thousands of people met in cinemas, coliseums, squares, parks, football stadiums, and hills; crutches, canes and orthopaedic devices were thrown away because of prayer, healing, and miracles. This unique period of revival lasted from August 1972 until February 1973. Its last meeting was held in La Paz on 21 January 1973, when the Hernando Siles Stadium was packed with 40,000 people inside and 22,000 outside. Ruibal preached and prayed for healing with both groups.[60]

The national and international press covered these events extensively. The Bolivian Bible Society sold all their Bibles and had to urgently order 33,000 Bibles from neighbouring countries. In addition, New Testaments and pamphlets were widely distributed at that time. People from all social classes went to listen to Ruibal and witness the miracles that occurred when he preached. Many of those who attended came from rural areas and could barely understand what was being preached in Spanish.[61] He received and accepted invitations to go to Peru, Ecuador, Brazil, Paraguay, and Colombia. However, youth groups remained in Bolivia, in La Paz, Cochabamba, and Santa Cruz to continue meeting and preaching. These groups ended up forming a movement with some of the characteristics of imported traditional Pentecostalism; but they also planted congregations and churches with a new, more autochthonous identity with national leadership, resources, structures, and organization. This was the start of Bolivian Neo-Pentecostalism.

This spiritual awakening ended in February 1973 in Bolivia and in November 1973 in Bogota, Colombia, when Ruibal went through a radical change in his life. Despite having received an invitation to preach alongside Kathryn Kuhlman in an evangelistic campaign in Jerusalem,[62] the young preacher decided to spend a month with a community of exclusive, legalistic Christians based in a country property near Bogota, the capital city of Colombia. It was in this community that he met his American wife, Ruth Johnson, in 1976. However, as a result of his contact with this group in 1973, Ruibal cut his hair and stopped wearing a white suit when preaching. On his

---

59. Ruibal, *Ungido para la cosecha del tiempo final*, 27, 33, 35.
60. De Calderon, *Porque el Senor asi lo promentio*, 63–70.
61. Ruibal, *Ungido para la cosecha del tiempo final*, 39.
62. Ruibal, 78.

return to Bolivia, he was a different person – consumed by legalism, having an excessive emphasis on rules, and demanding that his dwindling group of young converts observe his excessive adherence to traditionalist dress code. The young men were told to cut their hair and dress simply while the women had to wear long hair tied back in a ponytail, and skirts. He again held meetings in public places, but the impact and power observed in his previous revival was gone. The new group, in turn, split into three parts: those who faithfully observed Ruibal's imposed legalism, the "unfaithful", and those who went back to their previous lives.[63] In February 1974, Ruibal and a select group of young people who had accepted his strict rules organized a series of seven meetings that challenged people to choose between the pagan local Carnival festivities and a healing campaign in La Paz's main football stadium. This campaign gave rise to a group of converts who eventually formed the Bolivian Ekklesia Mission, a congregation of about 600 members, most of who are Aimara.[64] In July 1974, Ruibal left the newly established church in the care of some young leaders and moved to Colombia with his wife. They eventually broke away from the legalistic group in Bogota and moved to Cali, Colombia. There he started: the Colombian Ekklesia Christian Centre, which worked in education; the Latin American Christian University (UCLA); some radio stations; and a television channel. Ruibal, in his own words, said:

After more than 20 years of ministry, we now live in a simple rented house in the city of Cali. Once we had to sleep on the floor for nine months. I have no savings or investments and, until recently, my car was a 1968 Chevrolet. However, I enjoy the greatest benefits that come from God's favour.[65]

In December 1995, at the age of 42, Julio Cesar Ruibal was shot and killed when he was coming out of a Christian leaders' meeting in Cali. Some hired assassins shot him – allegedly over a dispute over a piece of land which Ruibal's organization had received as a donation upon which to build a church. Members of the local drug cartel also wanted the land. Ruibal previously had received several death threats and prophesied that his martyrdom would be a sacrifice for God's new time for Cali.

The film Transformations produced by Peter Wagner's spiritual warfare movement tells how Ruibal's death led to a group of about 200 pastors meeting every night to pray for the drug cartel to be dismantled.[66] They were convinced

---

63. De Calderon, *Porque el Senor asi lo prometio*, 120.
64. De Calderon, 22.
65. Ruibal, *Ungido para la cosecha del tiempo final*, 69.
66. Otis, *Transformations: A documentary*.

that spiritual forces controlled geographical locations and that Colombia's problems, with the drug trade, corruption, and violence, were caused by these spiritual forces. For Morrillo, this was a simplistic, spiritualized, biased reading of the situation that lacked Christian values and teaching about justice, poverty, reconciliation, and forgiveness.[67]

Westernized young people with middle-class values, like Julio Cesar Ruibal, helped bring South American Neo-Pentecostalism to birth and saw it flourish in Bolivia, mainly among Aimaras. Luis Guachalla, the founder and leader of the PoGC, openly says that it was Ruibal who introduced him to the Neo-Pentecostal faith when he was a young man from a middle-class background.[68] The transition of pre-modern societies from rural indigenous community life to modernity in the urban centres has led to the creation of a new religious identity for most Bolivians. However, because Bolivia is a predominantly poor country made up of majority indigenous groups, the Neo-Pentecostal movement reflects that composition with a predominant Aimara and Quechua membership.

Independent of Roman Catholicism and of reformed Protestantism (at least to begin with), Neo-Pentecostalism experienced enormous numerical growth and formed the largest urban churches. Revolving around the experience of the power of the Holy Spirit, almost all these early churches, with some exceptions like the Comercio Street Church in La Paz, emphasized miraculous healings, material prosperity, anti-intellectuality, and emotional ecstasy.

Summary

This reading of the history of the Aimaras, including the Aimaran Neo-Pentecostals, helps to understand their development and observe their present-day reality. The permanent symbioses of elements of different natures have favoured the development of an Aimaran identity without defined or closed profiles. What is observed are unions, modes, and tonalities within the Aimara that have mixed and overlapped. Their development processes reflect the crises, adaptation, and reconstruction lived by this people and culture – processes that have formed their identity today.

In the last century, two dynamic global movements have impacted Bolivian Aimaras – modernity and (since the 1970s) the new evangelical religious

---

67. Morillo, 'Critique of the transformations video'.
68. Guachalla, "Raices del Ministerio del Nuevo Pacto Poder de Dios".

movements[69], including the Neo-Pentecostals.[70] The revival led by Julio Cesar Ruibal, a Bolivian medical student, who held evangelistic campaigns and performed miracles in football stadiums and mining centres in the early 1970s was the origin of the Neo-Pentecostal movement.[71] This movement gave rise to what are now the biggest churches in Bolivia.

This new version of the Pentecostal church mainly attracts poor, indigenous people who live in outlying, peri-urban areas. Many are unemployed rural immigrants; their move to the city brings identity changes and, sometimes, social and economic mobility. Belonging to one of these churches is seen to be a step up the social ladder.[72] The silhouette of PoGC members has continuity with these historical facts and analogous characteristics that will be disclosed in the following chapter.

---

69. The word evangelical is used in Bolivia to describe what in other parts of the world is known as the Protestant Church. Phillips, Protestantism in Bolivia, 13. In this study the two words are used interchangeably.

70. Albó, "La experiencia religiosa Aymara," 322–323.

71. Riviere, "Bolivia: el pentecostalismo en la sociedad Aymara del Altiplano," 262.

72. Droogers 1991, "Visiones paradójicas sobre una religión paradójica," 21.

4

The Power of God Church

Introduction

An interactive encounter between meanings is taking place in the La Paz religious scenario where the PoGC makes use of its persuasive marketing style, with practices adapted to both old and new, urban and Aimara cultures. This meeting of meanings creates conflict and generates new identities. For Aimaran Neo-Pentecostals, this new identity involves new beliefs while maintaining indigenous elements, synthesized rituals, contextual social relationships, and re-interpreted ethical norms.

Pentecostalism has become a socio-religious expression that questions not only the traditional hegemonic monopoly of the benefits of salvation, but also social and cultural behaviours practised until today by both those who have adopted institutional Catholicism mixed with Aimara animism and those who consider themselves conservative evangelical Protestants. Marginalized urban populations in La Paz are turning to different religious practices, creating a heterogeneous religious scenario.

Populist Catholics (who follow a Catholicism of the people) and Pentecostal evangelicals are rival religious agents constantly competing for the same socio-religious universe and geographic area. They both appeal to populations that are socially and economically marginalized and respond to new religious consumer demands. With the

extraordinary growth of non-historic evangelical churches, particularly Pentecostal and Neo-Pentecostal churches, Latin America – home to 62 percent of the world's Catholics – is becoming less Catholic.

Pentecostalism in Latin America has been described as the Protestant version of populist Catholic religiosity.[1] It is populist not only because it attracts

---

1. Sepúlveda, "Pentecostalism as popular religiosity," 80.

the poor, but also because it moulds people's day-to-day way of life. The growth and influence of Neo-Pentecostalism in Bolivia occurs amid increased poverty for millions of people who find that the Neo-Pentecostal church apparently identifies with their suffering and their socio-religious world.

When the role of fiestas or festivals within populist urban Catholicism is considered, it is seen that fiestas fulfil a dual function. While being an outward expression of devotion to a "saint" or "virgin", they are also a mechanism for promoting someone within the social hierarchy. In other words, these religious fiestas are a mechanism for identifying and integrating the inhabitants of a given area, while also giving the wealthy social elite an opportunity to show off their social, cultural, and economic superiority. Work-related fiestas serve to recreate the identity of those who have immigrated to large cities. On studying the syncretism concerning fiestas, Albó distinguishes between a religious syncretism linked with Andean tradition and another type of syncretism related to power groups. Writing about the first, he says:

> Just as it is difficult to distinguish Christian aspects within the fiesta, it is also complicated to try to isolate the purely Andean elements that have been transformed or neutralized by two complementary factors: the historic factor of their Christianization and the more recent urbanization factor.[2]

Meanwhile, Guaygua says that urban Aimara Catholics in La Paz do not want to convert to Pentecostalism for two main reasons. First, Catholicism is the religion of their forefathers. It is the faith of their cultural tradition and, socially, it is the religion of their collective ancestors and relatives. Second, as a system of networks of reciprocities between relatives and accomplices – gods, saints, and people both alive and dead – the emphasis of Catholicism is in its value as a belief system and form of worship. It offers: a familiar experience, something sacred, and a form of faith lived out of affection which the Pentecostals came not only to deny but also to destroy.[3]

Populist Catholicism, therefore, (as expressed in fiestas) combines beliefs and rituals, integrating and adapting traditional Catholic and Aimaran values to powerfully attract the urban multitudes of the city of La Paz. It promotes socio-economic structures based on the form and logic of reciprocities associated with power, affection, rights, and obligations. It influences models of family, kinship, and the rules that govern friendship, traditional labor unions

---

2. Albó and Preiswerk, *Los senhores del Gran Poder*, 241.
3. Guaygua, "El mercado y los bienes de salvacion," 53,

and relationships between neighbours – following a concept closely linked to past and present rural religious practice. And in doing so it redefines and rebuilds identity.

While some tend to relate Pentecostalism to urban modernity, seeing conversion to a new religion as an effective means for adopting a Western lifestyle, others see it as an idealized reconstruction of traditional indigenous society.[4] In other words, for the uprooted and disorientated masses attempting to build new socio-cultural patterns in cities, Pentecostalism offers a substitute community that provides effective answers and solutions for the construction of a new identity. However, instead of separating the trend towards modernity from the trend towards the traditional indigenous world, Pentecostal practice and its message have elements of both continuity and discontinuity with people's forms of cultural and religious expression.

What, then, are the characteristics of Neo-Pentecostalism that explain its identity and work? What is happening specifically in the PoGC? This Neo-Pentecostal form of Bolivian Pentecostalism is operating mainly in urbanized sectors of La Paz that are poor, marginalized, and with strong indigenous roots. The poor people who attend the PoGC in La Paz live in areas where life is precarious and in recent years has become even more insecure and worthless. How does the Church handle the challenges faced daily by its members and leaders?

The PoGC in Its Environment

> Pentecostalism, rather than being a doctrine, proposes a particularly intense experience of God, capable of offering a "road to salvation" – new meaning to life – radically different from the biographic opportunities offered by society in general… It opens doors to an experience of God, without the need for mediation … It communicates a known, verbal and non-verbal language … The subject being announced is also a man of the people … It is nourished by the incorporation of a community of people that shares the experience and celebrates it in affective, effective solidarity with new believers.[5]

---

4. Garrard-Burnet, *Rethinking Protestantism in Latin America*.
5. Guaygua and Castillo, *Identidades y religion*, 77.

The context of the PoGC is peculiar to the indigenous and poor who are the majority population in the biggest city of the country. Located in the busiest area of La Paz with a high demographic density, the PoGC's main arena for generating a harvest from its evangelizing work is the "La casa de Dios" in Riosiño Square. This area is in the northwestern hillside of the Bolivian capital city; it is distinguished as being the most densely populated part of the city. This area is also home of participants of Señor del Gran Poder Fiesta, the main religious expression of populist Catholicism held once a year in May.[6] The parallelism between the name of the church that is "Power of God", the geographic area's name, "Great Power", and the urban well-liked Catholic fiesta name "Lord of Great Power" are probably not a coincidence.

More probably, it reveals a prevalent thread that unites cultural, religious, geographic, and social aspects of the Aimara who live there. People come from many different poor neighbourhoods to attend the church meetings in the area. The area is typified by very needy social sectors: a neglected and abandoned population; a context marked by crisis, conflict, and contrasts; low-income levels; precarious employment; and limited access to basic services. This is the reality lived in this part of La Paz and, in turn, by the church congregation.

The Atmosphere of Worship Services

The first of the six Sunday services held in the PoGC starts early – just as the lives of the Aimaran people living in La Paz and the Sunday street sellers in the Gran Poder Area start before dawn. The main church building opens while it is still dark as people are already arriving at 4:30 a.m. A worship and praise time starts before 6:00 a.m., by which time the building has standing room only. In fact, the building is set out for the congregation to stand throughout to allow the maximum number of people to attend each service. Four rows of seats are laid out on the right-hand-side of the colourful building, earmarked for the elderly and those in poor health. Otherwise, people stand throughout the services, which usually last for over three hours. The most popular service – for both congregation and pastor – is the early Sunday morning service.

The soloist who leads the music gradually moves from quiet invitations to worship to more lively praise songs set to rhythms based on Latin pop, and then, in turn, to Bolivian and Colombian cumbia-style music with the singing growing increasingly louder and more effusive. This progressive preparation lasts for 90–120 minutes, building up to the moment for Pastor Guachalla's

---

6. Albó and Preiswerk, *Los senhores del Gran Poder*, 5, 113.

appearance. His arrival is the focus point for everyone's attention and signals the beginning of two of the most important parts of the service – the appeal for tithes and offerings and the delivery of the message.

During the last half-hour of the praise time about fifty uniformed ushers, men and women, stand with their backs to the stage like a squadron of soldiers. They line up ready for their work to begin as soon as the pastor appears. Fifty ushers is quite a high number for a congregation of 500–600, but they have to move through the untidy rows of people, passing out blessed offering and tithe envelopes printed with the church logo and motto, making sure that no-one refuses to receive one.

Pastor Guachalla's church motto is a short phrase taken from the Bible, which he sprinkles liberally throughout his appeals and sermons, often in crescendo tones; it is like a talisman, capable of stirring the congregation to feverish heights. "Because nothing is impossible for God" the pastor says. "Because nothing is impossible for God", the congregation repeats effusively. The pastor adorns the motto with phrases that create a collective sense of comfort, excitement, stupor, and absence of any critical spirit. For the congregations, the church building appears to become the only place on Earth – and the pastor knows he has them where he wants them.

At eight o'clock in the morning the pastor knows from experience that he has prepared the ground for his malleable flock. He subsequently moves straight to the point: he asks them for their offerings using two symbols from the Aimara worldview – reciprocity and retribution for the yatiri. At this crucial point in the Sunday morning services, he makes use of the practices of an Aimaran religious agent to ask for cash contributions from the church members. He ties the giving of offerings to the people's understanding of native cultural performances.

One member is already waiting near the platform to be invited to join the pastor who then embraces him and commends him for his US$1,000 offering. The pastor has the money in his right-hand pocket; he now takes it out, holds it in the air, then counts the green notes slowly one by one, "100, 200, 300…900, 1000." Pastor Guachalla then tells the congregation: "For his generosity, this brother will receive a crown of gold in heaven. Do you want to receive a crown of gold? Or maybe one of tin or, even worse, paper?" He asks them how much they plan to give this morning and asks them to give more. He teases them, urging them to give more if they do not want the congregation to laugh at their crown. He warns that the US$1000-donor will laugh from his seat in heaven on seeing that they do not have a golden prize.

With his words, his mimicry, and by using different types of voice, the pastor by now has everyone laughing. The message is clear: the more you give to the PoGC, the more you will receive under the Aimara's principle of reciprocity. The more you give to the Church, the more you will receive from God. This is the backbone of the Aimara's communal, religious, and cultural belief in reciprocity.

The crowd's response is slow. Some begin to open their blessed envelopes to add a little more cash. The pastor reminds those who own their homes that God gave them that gift without them doing anything to deserve it. He tells those who live in rented property that it is God who gave them that roof over their heads. He ends by asking if they, who have homes to live in, are going to leave God without resources. This is another appeal that penetrates the fibres of native worldview. If God has given to us, will we, in turn, not give to him?

Pastor Guachalla suddenly stops speaking to the standing congregation – by now doing some mental arithmetic to see if they can afford to give more – and turns his eyes to the building roof to show that he is addressing God and to make clear what he has said. He prays for those who do not believe, for those whom the devil has blinded so that they will not give sacrificially, for those who have quickly forgotten how much they have received, and for those who could still receive a crown of gold! He then interrupts his communication with God to hold a final ritual before the ushers collect the offerings.

Imitating a yatiri, Pastor Guachalla orders everyone to put their envelopes on the left-hand side of their chest close to the heart. In field research, I saw the testimony of a seller in focus group Seven, who described how the yatiri, before asking for payment, asked him to put the money close to his heart to show that their decision to give is made with all their feelings. If they want great things, if they seek great things, they must give sacrificially to receive the best.

Here the pastor makes a short parenthesis to explain that the "House of God" construction in one of the city's most densely populated areas cost approximately US $2,000,000. "Because nothing is impossible for God" is chorused by the congregation. As the uniformed ushers make their tortuous route through the standing faithful, they collect what will be the first of five bountiful Sunday collections.

The PoGC has become rich and powerful by adopting and adapting the indigenous channels of reciprocity and relationality regarding the transcendent. It uses syncretistic practice regarding how divine favours are paid for – and for which the Aimara language and worldview are powerful tools. The PoGC owns a network of radio stations in each capital city and a television network that broadcasts nationally in addition to premises in prime areas that are easy for the population to access. Although nobody is forced to give, the church services use mechanisms to exploit people's innocence and lack of information. The church uses an abusive induction. The same method is used in mass media meetings or musical concerts. The masses are manipulated using emotionalism and exploiting people's ignorance, belief system, and poverty.

Before starting his sermon, the pastor allows a few people to give testimonies of healing miracles. Time is short now, but the much-awaited message has still to come. One person shares about healing from chronic anaemia that stopped him from walking or even thinking. Others talk of the desperate urban misery experienced since moving to the city. When leaving the temple after three-and-a-half hours of intensive performance, I see there are other people with chronic anaemia and extreme poverty in the corridors. People in need are lying on the pavement – looking for an opportunity for a Pentecostal-animist solution to their problems, or at least some help.

Communication Modes

The ethos of this church incorporates several lines of thought: new and traditional beliefs associated with new and traditional social lifestyles; urban and rural customs; and rhetorical uses of popular language. These three factors are enveloped in cultural forms that range from native Aimara to marginalized urban immigrant. Although the spoken and ritualized contents reflect considerable ambiguity and contradiction, there is a strong sense of building something new, of creating a new life and identity based on their situations and possibilities.

Bible use in the PoGC is ritualistic rather than exegetic. A large majority of members are either completely illiterate or have limited reading skills meaning that the Bible is used in an emphatically symbolic manner – more as an object than as an inspirational subject of belief and conviction. No questions are asked regarding rituals neither do rituals leave room for discussion. The partakers simply observe the rituals: they believe that being there guarantees the salvation of the world. The simple act of placing the Bible in the pulpit, or on the sick or demon-possessed, represents the action of liberating forces. The repetition of passages from the Old or New Testament attracts – or so it is believed – invisible forces that are almost magical. So, the Bible – along with other ritualized practices used by the Neo-Pentecostals working among the poor – is related to forms and contents inherited from their ancestral universe that are relevant to their socio-economic needs.

The meetings at the PoGC reflect a circle of repetition, both in form and content, in established times and spaces. Although the services appear to be spontaneous, every setting is carefully planned. The leader and people behave in a special, organized, religious, and cultural way that pleases everybody by fascinating, surprising, and disturbing them.

Since translation into Aimara has gradually been incorporated into the PoGC services in recent years, these events have become very popular and are repeatedly broadcast via the PoGC radio and television stations. The church building is decorated indoors with colourful flags, bright walls, and a multi-coloured set-up, reflecting the Aimaras' love for bright colours as seen, for example, in how they dress. These uses of the Aimara language, the colourful scenario, community life, and many other distinctive Aimaran aspects give the PoGC its resultant indigenous Aimaran character.

Aimaran Neo-Pentecostals associate the Christian faith with the religious world of the poor. This association has more to do with the religious experience and vision of the indigenous culture than with urbanized Western culture. Pentecostalism is based on religious experience more than doctrine; it proposes an ecstatic experience of God that offers solutions, salvation, a new identity, and meaning to life. Members are empowered. They experience God in a factual way and communicate the miracles they experience every day to people from their own culture in their own language. Joining a community of people who share the same understandings and experiences – and celebrating these things together– affectively and effectively strengthens the Aimaran Pentecostal experience.

History – How Did the PoGC Start?

Pastor Luis Guachalla, founder and indisputable leader, answers to this question mentioning his own conversion experience:

> I am one of Julio Cesar Ruibal's sheep. I was not converted in a church. I was converted by [listening to the] radio. That night when Julio Cesar Ruibal preached, I accepted Jesus and was converted. Your heart, your mind, changes. I gave myself to Jesus right then in Yungas [tropical region near La Paz]. I only wanted to talk about Jesus. I wanted to leave that place and go to La Paz.[7]

---

7. Guachalla, *Raices del Ministerio del Nuevo Pacto Poder de Dios*.

In a taped message given at the Sunday service on 9 November 2003, Guachalla told the congregation how the ministry of the New Power of God Covenant Church started twenty years earlier with his conversion. The radio station he listened to in 1983 was Radio Illimani. Guachalla tells how, three months after his conversion, he was preaching in Perez Velasco, the busiest area in central La Paz, alongside Jhonny Vasquez, Fermin Caso, and their families. Mr and Mrs Guachalla trained to become soul-winners in the toughest part of town.

After schooling, Guachalla spent a few years at university studying law and agronomy. When he was twenty, he married Magnely – now also a pastor in the PoGC – and they had two children. Their son is currently a youth leader in the church and their daughter sings and presents television programmes for children. The family has a high-profile leadership role in an organization that now has twenty-two churches, twenty radio stations, and a television channel with an impact throughout the country and abroad.[8]

Pastor Guachalla describes the phases of the PoGC ministry as "visionary pregnancies." Each time he has a new vision, he says, he feels like a pregnant woman about to give birth. First, it was the Radio Sol (or the Sun Radio Station), then television Channel 45, and then it was what church members call the *terrenazo*, a large plot of land in the Riosiño Square area where the costly "House of God" is being built as the PoGC headquarters and church building.

The media stations play a key role in church growth. The PoGC's Radio Sol, bought in 1990, captures a huge audience with what is called an "open tribunal" where Aimaran believers can testify of the supposed miracles experienced in their lives. The television channel follows a similar broadcasting style.

When the "Jesus Tent" outreach ended its touring ministry in 1988 Pastor Guachalla started using cinema buildings for church services, moving from one cinema to another in La Paz's busy, commercial Gran Poder neighbourhood. He borrowed money to pay for musical instruments and to rent the cinemas that provided him with the necessary platforms for church services. He paid to air his radio programmes and then, with the help of a German-born tourist known as Ali, he moved from the Cine Madrid to the Cine Esmeralda, then to the Cine Mexico before bringing the PoGC headquarters to the previous Cine Roby.

---

8. Ministry of the New Power of God Covenant, "Gran avivamiento de Bolivia a las naciones."

Pastor Luis Guachalla

Guachalla firmly places himself as the centre of the birth, growth, and continuity not only of the church, but the entire ministry of the New Power of God Covenant. PoGC members are convinced that this is Guachalla's rightful position. After working hard with an itinerant ministry in the 1980s, Guachalla started leading a "spiritual revival" in the 1990s, attracting crowds of people who were looking for healing, and performing all kinds of miracles. Guaygua and Castillo write about Guachalla's beginnings in their recent comparative study of Neo-Pentecostalism and popular Catholicism in the city of El Alto:

> Pastor Guachalla's preaching bursts onto the scenario with a huge impact particularly among poorer segments of the population. By 2007, he had 10 churches in different regions, including El Alto, all with Bolivian pastors, becoming a national church that supports itself with its members' tithes and offering.[9]

Pastor Guachalla's personal charisma keeps him and his family in fixed control of the churches' theological-doctrinal, economic, and social patrimony. His visionary "pregnancies" set the boundaries for the path taken by the PoGC and all that implies. He is the decision-maker; he defines important and minor rules. It was his idea to build a mega church, which would then reproduce many other dependent churches. Pastor Guachalla lays the guidelines for media use, finances, organisation, administration, and defining the church's structure and style. There is no accountability system – no board to whom Guachalla can give an account or by which his ministry can be evaluated.

Theological Orientation of the Church

The PoGC theoretically upholds that salvation is not lost, following the Calvinist school of thought. In practice, however, the church's repeated, often dramatic appeals to its members to convert seem to throw doubt on the doctrine of eternal salvation and perhaps are a strategy to keep people in the church and ensure that they really change their religion. Although the pastor says that they are saved, the ordinary church members believe that they need to convert again when they experience problems, lack of faith, sin, or temptation. There are various doctrines that are important for the POGC's theology and practice.

---

9. Guaygua and Castillo, *Identidades y religion*, 84.

Spiritual Warfare
This means that the church and the believers are in an intense battle against their enemy, the devil. This being leads an army of demons who are to be found everywhere, seeking to discourage or tempt the believer to sin.

Prosperity Theology
This teaches that the believer has a right to be wealthy and enjoy the riches of the modern capitalist world. The more money the believer gives to the church, the more he or she will receive from God. This doctrine also teaches that Christians should be healthy and that if a Christian suffers from some physical illness, this is due to sin or lack of faith.

Baptism in the Holy Spirit
The PoGC teaches that, in addition to receiving salvation, the believer must also be filled with the Holy Spirit – a condition that occurs when the person shakes all over and speaks in strange tongues.

Pre- and Post-Millennialist Eschatology
Pre- and post-eschatology seem to co-exist in the PoGC in that the church expects the rapture to occur in the last times amidst the final tribulation so that believers are taken to be with Jesus Christ in heaven; however, it also believes that the church can bring the kingdom of God to Earth by improving the world progressively until the millennium reign of Christ begins.

Structure and Organisation

Mr and Mrs Guachalla are ultimately responsible for the church's theological and economic administration, with the support of a select group of trusted colleagues who have been trained, not in seminary, but in the aggressive forms of evangelism practiced by the PoGC. They must, for example, have worked in Soul Winners (SW) cell groups and preached in the streets, prisons, and hospitals. Some of the best leaders are delegated with the task of starting daughter churches in other neighbourhoods, provinces, or departments where the PoGC ministry does not yet have a strong presence. The church's organisational structure, therefore, is simple: Pastor Guachalla and his wife are at the head, followed by men and women pastors from other congregations in La Paz and other parts of Bolivia, then the intermediate leaders who run the SW cell groups and worship groups, and finally the ordinary church members.

Leadership

The pastors and SW leaders focus their work on three areas: preaching the word of God, prayer, and fasting. They also visit any members of their congregation or cell group with health, economic, or family problems. They only have practical training without formal theological studies therefore they preach spur-of-the-moment sermons, believing the Holy Spirit uses them. The Neo-Pentecostal PoGC leader is accountable to the mother church, training and ministering in the SW cell groups because that there is where leaders receive God's call and the gift for ministry. Each leader's main objective is to extend the work of Pastor Guachalla. Most of these leaders are so enthusiastic about their calling that they work fulltime without any economic payment.

The PoGC leadership is predominantly male although, in recent years, an attempt has been made to include women. The majority of members are women, comprising up to 70 percent of SW home groups and churches, however less than 10 percent of all associate pastors in the whole country are women. Being an associate pastor means being paid; the number of them is small in relation to the whole structure of the church. Most women leaders are unpaid lay leaders.

Women also make up the majority of those involved in evangelistic endeavours. This was verified on several opportunities at the church services, at the radio and television stations, and in the marketplace where Radio Sol is listened to by women church members as they sell their wares.

Social Character of the Church

The social component of the PoGC is largely homogeneous in terms of Aimaran culture and social class, but the select leadership group is predominantly white rather than indigenous. A small group of middle-class members exercises considerable influence on the majority membership. A significant part of the PoGC membership also attends other evangelical churches. They continue to attend the PoGC out of a sense of loyalty or interest, but like to go round trying out other alternatives.

Soul Winners Cell Groups

Through the "Soul Winners" (SW) groups the PoGC spreads its message to other families and neighbourhoods. The PoGC estimates that there are about 5,000 SW groups holding weekly meetings in homes in different parts of

Bolivia; these home meetings reproduce on a small scale the atmosphere of preaching, worship, and prayer found in the main PoGC church.

The cell groups are usually led by the hosts who open their homes to relatives and friends in order to share a truth that will transform their inner lives and make them break away from the practices of the world. New converts are introduced to a new lifestyle and conduct without any bad habits, like drinking alcohol. This religious micro-cosmos is the informal, but effective, school that trains church members so that they, in turn, can become leaders of similar cell groups that focus on people's souls and their spiritual needs, without seeing the whole person. The SW groups are also the raw material used for forming new congregations.

Testimonies of the Church Members

The testimonies obtained in this study show that the PoGC ministry focuses on two main areas: healing and offerings. On listening to PoGC members' testimonies in the church building or on TV Channel 45, it is apparent that the main modus operandi is the interview led by Pastor Luis Guachalla. He asks the questions, controls the microphone, and leads the person giving his or her testimony to say what he needs them to say to confirm his teaching.

At one side of the stage, Guachalla's wife and a group of pastors select the people who will be given the privilege of sharing from the many people who want to give witness to what God is doing in their lives. The chosen ones, with Guachalla's prompting, tell of their experience of healing or prosperity in a dramatic life-or-death tone of voice. While people share their testimonies, two levels of participation are observed in the congregation. On the one hand, ordinary church members are given the chance to speak about a miracle in their lives and have their voice heard in the congregation while, on the other, Pastor Luis Guachalla prompts the rest of the congregation to repeatedly chant one of the PoGC's favourite slogans: "Nothing is impossible for God".

Worship

Each church service includes lots of singing, some led by Bolivian folk groups who play Andean-type music, and some led by electronic bands who play salsas, *cumbias* (popular Colombian music), *rancheras* (popular Mexican music), and Latin pop music. When the bands start to sing the different praise and worship songs the church members are encouraged to sing along, raise their hands, dance, and get excited.

More than six musicians using the best of sound technology lead the congregation in worship for what is the longest segment of the service, with the music usually lasting well over an hour. This praise time is vital for the Church's objectives as it serves to communicate joy, optimism, and hope, and prepares the way for the next sixty minutes of offerings and preaching.

The Mission of the PoGC: Interviews with Members and Leaders

Field exploration demonstrates that the ordinary church members and intermediate-level leaders in the PoGC, both young people and adults, adopt new forms of thinking. These new ways of thinking are reflected in their identity, their acceptance duty to fulfil the POGC's task and objectives, and their changed daily routines after conversion. Now, all consider themselves sent and empowered to look for new converts along with submission to church leadership and structure.

This section of qualitative analysis is based on twenty-nine in-depth interviews with fifteen intermediate-level leaders (cell groups and worship) and fourteen ordinary church members. Each interview lasted about an hour and focused on the following five areas, with open exchange and discussion between the interviewer and interviewee:

1. Perception of the personal conversion experience
2. Experience related to the mission of the believer
3. Concepts about the mission of the believer
4. Experiences in evangelism and discipleship
5. Opinions about integral mission.

Perception of Personal Conversion Experience
Ordinary Members
Metamorphosis with profound changes in their lifestyle and concepts about life is the experience of PoGC believers after conversion. The reconstruction of mental, emotional, and spiritual concepts as a result of approaching and joining the PoGC church is shared by ordinary members and intermediate leaders. Ordinary members born in rural areas talked about previous emotional states, such as looking for happiness or feeling themselves drawn into the urban flurry of drunkenness and parties. People with Aimaran roots, but born in urban areas, had a different perspective about their conversion. Several had joined

the PoGC after being baptized in other evangelical churches. Some had been Baptists or part of another large Neo-Pentecostal church in La Paz, Cristo Viene (Christ is Coming), where, they said, the Holy Spirit was absent and there was a bad testimony. For both groups, conversion had meant no more drinking, no more participation in parties, and no visits to Aimaran religious men, like yatiris.

The following two testimonies belong to a man and a woman, ordinary PoGC church members, who have been attending the church for more than two years:

> I was converted three years ago. Since I was a policeman, it was more difficult for me, because I thought being a policeman was bad. My wife understood me and forgave me. I don't drink any more, I don't argue. There are no more fights, drunkenness, and insults. I have not left the Lord because the Word of God says that apart from God, we can do nothing.
>
> I was going through a tough time in my family. I was thinking about committing suicide. Someone invited me to church, and I accepted Jesus there. That was in December 2000. My life changed. Now I don't participate in the dance groups any longer. I went to talk to my relatives to ask for forgiveness and forgive. I never used to do that because I was too proud. I share about my conversion with other people. I tell them about what I was going through before. I share in my work, with relatives and with people whenever I get the chance.

On talking about their conversion, interviewees emphasized physical healing they had received and their lifestyle prior to conversion. Their reasons for belonging to the PoGC were often associated with healing miracles that they themselves or close relatives, like a spouse and children, had experienced. They tended to speak in more detail about their life before conversion than about their present routine explaining, for example, "I used to do the stuff everybody else does," "before I used to go to the yatiri for everything," "I used to fight and shout a lot," "I went from party to party, to yatiris, witches," "I drank a lot, wasted my money," "I was about to commit suicide." These are some of the repeated expressions found in the interviews. This list of past behaviours is not unchangeable and rigid, but flexible, under constant revision and restructuring, forming an identity that is not entirely new, but differs from the old one while still being built on their indigenous ethnicity.

Intermediate Leaders

How do two of the young Aimara intermediate leaders describe their conversion experience? The two belong to different worship groups; one in an Andean music group, and another in an electronic group. Let's see what they say remembering that they have been in the congregation for a long time:

> I received Christ in 1999. My mother talked to me about the Word. It was a miracle. I never knew what a miracle was before, but since I met God, I learned that only God can do miracles. Before things went badly for me at work, now they don't. Since then, lots of things have changed, for example, my character. I used to be very rebellious with my mum, I never obeyed her. I liked dancing. The year I was converted I was about to participate in a folkloric parade, but I didn't. I never went to consult yatiris but I visited the Socavón [mine entrance where people worship the Virgin Mary and the devil] in the Oruro Carnival parade and I used to pray to the saints.
>
> I received Christ five years ago at a time when I had many problems. My wife had lost our baby and, as a result, my life was out of control. I came to know Christ, and everything changed because both of us received God. We no longer went to parties, we didn't go to the big parades, but we had never visited a yatiri.

When talking about their conversion experience young leaders focus on changes in character and conduct. They talk about the fact that they no longer participate in religious festivals or attend social gatherings where alcohol is served. They emphasize the sentimental aspect of their conversion – the change of heart. Adult leaders, on the other hand, focus on new moral values. Those with prior experience in grassroots organizations practice their leadership skills learned outside the church – in unions, mothers' clubs, or neighbourhood associations – by working within the Church, helping the administration, being SW cell group leaders, or assisting in radio programming. Another generational difference is the relationship with Aimaran/Andean beliefs, religious agents, and post-conversion. The young people tend to adhere much less than adults to the Aimaran worldview and animistic rituals, having adopted the globalized vision transmitted in urban centres. In both age groups, male and female members all express that the sharing of the testimony of their conversion with friends and relatives is a powerful instrument for disseminating their new faith.

Experience Related to the Mission of the Believer
Ordinary Members

The Neo-Pentecostal faith clearly gives each convert the unavoidable responsibility to share and expand the particular Neo-Pentecostal way of understanding and living their faith, as if it were unique and superior. All the people interviewed expressed that they had found a meaning for life, a greater purpose, which they described as "serving the Lord," "preaching," "telling people to repent," "talking about the Lord," "winning souls from hell," "God heals, I tell them…" Each testimony is part of a concept and experience of mission that applies to men and women, young and old.

Although all those interviewed include in their new perception the desire to share their new world view in the areas where they live, in the country, and the world, newer converts accept this challenge without joining neighbourhood associations or other socio-political groups. Older converts, on the other hand, both men and women, are much more open to participating in grassroots organizations. Both groups, however, separate the practice of their faith from any form of serving others. Their physical and spiritual energy, their financial resources, and their personal assets are for their own and the church's use rather than for meeting the needs of others. Apart from praying for divine healing, the PoGC tends to defer material needs to a secondary plane.

In the following testimonies, some members describe their understanding of the mission of the believer:

> Since my conversion, my life's purpose has been to serve the Lord and tell everyone about the gospel. I do not have any specific plans for my family, just for them to know the Lord and not to suffer in this world. My plan is that everyone in my neighbourhood converts to the gospel and I share with all types of people in order to reach that goal.
>
> We go out in the streets to play music, to evangelize. We attend house group meetings; we go out visiting. When I'm not working, I come to fast; there are fasting meetings in the church every day. I feel more at ease when I come to fast, when I come to church. Everyone in my house have been converted, little by little. First my wife, then my children. For my daughter it is more difficult, she is not converted, but she is beginning to understand and I'm happy about that … My life's purpose is to win souls for the Lord so that they do not go to hell.

Other activities described by the interviewees as part of their mission include handing out tracts, ushering at church services, prayer, fasting, evangelizing in the streets and public squares, and hospital visiting. Their new lifestyle often earns them criticism and rejection from relatives and neighbours.

Intermediate Leaders

One phrase that the interviewees, young and old, repeat when referring to their mission is "saving souls." This, they say, is their life's purpose. Worship group leaders via their music and SW cell group leaders via teaching in their groups clearly specify that their priority focuses on people's souls. Young leaders show complete indifference to the social aspects of their faith, limiting themselves to being an example of solidarity and honesty in the workplace. Adults who have previous experience in grassroots organizations, on the contrary, talk about having been, and in some cases still being, part of neighbourhood or shop-owner organizations; they also participate in campaigns to give used clothing and other articles to the poor.

Again, the following testimonies from young Aimaran leaders reflect the focus of their mission:

> My life's purpose is to save my soul. There would be no sense for me to have a profession or wealth if I do not save my soul, [because] I would not go to be with God. In the short-term, I want to have a profession [usually means finishing a university degree] so that I can give my brothers and sisters what my parents couldn't give them. In the medium-term, I want to have a family and preach the word of God; in the long-term, I want to have a ministry, but guided always by my pastor. Plans for my neighbourhood include holding campaigns, activities to win them: dinners, food, show films … reach places where [the gospel] has not reached. The church has a mission and a vision. The mission is to win souls; the vision is to convert them to God.
>
> The purpose I have for my life is to be saved so that when God comes, I can go with Him. That is why one of my long-term goals is to become a pastor. In the short and medium term, my goal is to continue with the gospel beside my family and compose some songs for God. I have no plans for my neighbourhood because the people are very strange, and I have no relationship with them. At work, I want to continue talking to them about God to avoid them being envious of each other. In my church, I want to carry

on winning souls. That is the mission of every Christian in his or her church, to help people who are in a bad way.

The mission described by these respondents seems to be isolated from their social, political, and economic environments, even from the religious context, as it fails to take any other type of faith into consideration. It is a mission almost exclusively focused on spiritual aspects, essentially practised inside the nuclear and extended family. Almost all of those interviewed talked about successfully sharing their new way of life and faith with family members and workmates.

Experiences of Evangelism and Discipleship
Ordinary Members

The commitment to evangelize is deeply rooted in all those interviewed, whether they have been in the church for a long or a short time. However, what does evangelism mean for these people? Evangelizing for them means guiding others to go to church to hear the gospel and telling friends, relatives, neighbours, and workmates about how to know the good news of Jesus Christ. Convincing men and women to attend church, to listen to Radio Sol, or to watch TV Channel 45 is the main goal. In addition to the use of mass media, PoGC members also contribute to church growth by telling others about the miracles that have occurred both inside and outside the church. One Aimara woman, born in the rural area, said, "I share the gospel with everyone all the time. I have guided many people to take the first steps. I don't remember how many because I no longer have any contact with them." Another young indigenous woman, also born in the country, said, "I share the gospel with everyone and give out tracts, but I've never done any follow-up with anyone." One married man also born in the rural area said, "I share the gospel at work with my workers at break time. Sometimes they have problems, so I preach to them. I also talk to my relatives about the Lord." Another woman, born in the city, said "I always preach when I get the chance because that is my job. I share with my customers, my colleagues in the market, relatives, and neighbours."

Believers who have assisted in the congregation for less than two years appear to invite a much larger circle of friends and acquaintances. Their new faith makes them more daring and less selective about who they invite. Older believers, on the other hand, tend to prefer sharing with a more intimate circle of relatives and close friends or workmates. Newer converts are seen to be more intense about "sharing" their faith, while older believers show more perseverance and strategy in their mission work.

Intermediate Leaders

The head of church administration, who also leads the SW cell groups and a local shopkeepers' organization, said the following when talking about evangelism and discipleship:

> I constantly share the gospel with my family, friends, people I don't know. To the people who come to church and ask for help, whether they're Christians or not, the doors are always open for everyone. I tell them that there's a God who can change our lives, who can help us be born again and be new but in Jesus Christ. We go out to the streets with the pastor to preach the word in the squares, hospitals; everyone must do it because they want to without any conditions. I guide the new converts into Soul Winners groups and the meetings I have with shopkeepers. Each experience is important to me because each one is another life for God. In every experience my pastor helps me.

Cell group leaders as well as adults who previously belonged to grassroots organizations say they have led many people to conversion. This is not the case with worship group leaders and adults who have never participated in social organizations. All of them, however, are committed to bringing new people into the PoGC. One phrase used frequently in the interviews is "saving souls from hell" and this would seem to project their own need before conversion, their own sense of having been in hell. Even those who had been members of conservative evangelical churches before joining the PoGC – churches with little preaching about miracles, ecstatic experiences, and the gifts of the Holy Spirit – talk about only truly knowing God when they felt his power in the PoGC church.

> I have only shared the gospel with my brothers and sisters. I have had no experience with friends and people who are not Christians. Neither have I had the opportunity to guide a new convert in taking the first steps because I still have much to learn. I need to know more about the word, I need to have a stronger foundation in the word. I will do it when I have acquired more knowledge… The church should not only work to save souls from hell so that everyone can be saved.

As with ordinary members, intermediate PoGC leaders also share the good news about miracles with their extended families in the first place, and then their friends and workmates; however they go further, talking to neighbours, mothers' clubs, schools, and universities. They talk to others about what they believe God has done through supernatural deeds in the streets, in the church, with people they do not know, with drug users, the sick, couples contemplating divorce – every day and everywhere. They often evoke the pastor's key role in completing their evangelism or discipleship work, although the latter activity is much less common. Discipleship is basically understood as the continuous indoctrination of the convert and is rarely practised or even mentioned in comparison with convincing people to attend church or share a testimony of healing. The purpose of their life is to "win souls" which implies making that initial decision without worrying too much about what comes after. One young worship group leader said:

> I share the word at all times, whether at work, with neighbours, family, strangers. I talk to them about the word of God, telling them my testimony and talking to them about the Bible. In the word of God it says: "This gospel will be preached to every creature". That is an order from Jesus and I obey it without looking for anything in return. Any reward I get is God's blessing on my business and the experience with people who are just becoming Christians. You can share with them and usually the results are good. Those who are converted are always in the church.

Opinions about Integral Mission

Ordinary Members

"We have to enhance the Aimara culture without accepting idolatry and traditions," "we must recover things in the culture," "Aimara culture is of the devil," "we should think about the country's development," "the pastor has told us not to get involved in politics." These, sometimes contradictory, opinions were expressed by individual church members and appear to be spontaneous, changeable, and paradoxical observations rather than ongoing, well-thought-out reasoning or reflection.

Church members intrinsically understand identification with the poor and sensitivity to the cultural context (expounded as vital for "integral mission"[10]) because they are or have been poor and they come from the Aimaran culture.

---

10. Padilla, Misión Integral, 191. René Padilla defines the church's integral mission as: "Evangelization and social responsibility are inseparable. The gospel is the good news about the Kingdom of God. Good works, on the other hand, are the signs of the Kingdom for which we were created in Jesus Christ. Words and actions are indissolubly united in the mission of

The sensitivity and concern felt by poor Christians about the unemployed, the hungry, the poor, those who are vulnerable to – and often exploited by – the injustices of a segregationist system do not stem so much from a reflective awareness about these issues, as from an empathy for having shared the same suffering and the same indigenous identity. Their Neo-Pentecostal commitment and change occur within this indigenous socioeconomic reality. An elderly woman, born in the rural area, said, 'I have very little money, but if I had some, I would help all the children and poor people so that they do not suffer.' A new convert also said, "The church should work to save souls and seek God first and then it should worry about society, the poor, and the orphans and work for them; but our faith should be founded on Christ alone."

New converts seem to make a temporary clean break with politics, culture, and any activity that implies participation in society. An older convert, on the other hand, said, "We can participate in the neighbourhood committee by choice" and another woman expressed the belief that "the church should contribute to the country's development and the Aimara culture, but condemn idolatry", meaning that they must leave the worship of images, saints from Catholic background, ancestors, and gods from Aimara religion. These opinions reflect a substantial shift from the initial emotional charge experienced on the threshold of conversion.

Older converts, both male and female, expressed a desire to strengthen, improve, and recover aspects of their Aimaran culture, while emphatically rejecting idolatrous practices. They share aspirations of betterment, improvement, and rescuing the Aimaran culture. This could reflect a desire to preserve something precious and intimate or it could reflect the need for continuity and preservation.

Intermediate Leaders
Very few middle-level leaders still believe that the church's mission is only "to save souls from hell" or that "the Aimaran culture is of the devil. Although they acknowledge that the church does not address social issues, choosing to prioritize soul-saving, they recognize the importance for balance in Christian mission – a balance that clearly separates saving souls and the church's social responsibility. Evangelism is most important, but the believer should also contribute to Bolivia's progress, to enhancing Aimaran culture with the gospel, helping the poor, working for a better future for Bolivia, and eliminating

---

Jesus and his apostles and we should keep them together in the church's mission, in which Jesus' mission is prolonged until the end of time."

class discrimination. This radical separation between evangelism and social issues, relegating the latter to an inferior plane, is justified using the following explanations: "By evangelizing we form good people who value life," "winning souls is development for the country," "it is helping so that many people are not living in the streets," and "it is getting people out of vice so that they are useful for society."

Although the concept of an integral mission says that Christian faith has an impact on every part of human lives, adopting the concept may cause a Western-style dichotomy between what is spiritual and what is social. Aimara members of this Church do not have this dichotomy in everyday life. When talking about integral mission, they identify with their ecclesial context because they are poor people from indigenous communities. Young and adult intermediate leaders almost unanimously agree that they should value their Aimaran culture, speak their Aimara language, reject some of the negative customs, but retain solidarity, companionship, music, and traditional dress. The Aimaran culture is part of them and, they believe, the church should recreate that culture. The following quotes give some insight into Christians' vision of their Aimaran culture:

> The pastor teaches us that speaking Aimara is not a sin. It is true that indigenous people consult yatiris, have contact with them, but, in my church, we are going to change that. There are lots of Aimara-speaking people who go to the church, they are going to change that.
>
> The church should emphasize rescuing souls from hell more, but it should also be concerned about the nation's progress and helping the poor. With the arrival of the Spanish, they brought lots of customs that were foreign to us and they brought Christianity. But the Aimara culture is not evil, it is good. We must rescue things like the Aimara language so many people are ashamed of, and we should hold onto customs like the *apthapi*, that is, friendship and solidarity between brothers and sisters and staying away from things that do not please God.

Conclusion

In his study about the traditional religion of the Karamojon in East Africa, Knighton, who avoids a Western view and adopts an anthropological-historical approach, rediscovers the vitality of this native religion, reaching findings similar to those detected in this thesis about Aimaran Neo-Pentecostalism:

> Thus the vitality of traditional Karamojong religion continues, not so much the legitimation of a certain social structure as the heart of a culture, living by the faith of its people. In this the Karamojong are not of a strange order: it is just that they repeatedly invent their communities in unusual continuity with their past in order to preserve their autonomy for the future. They are not in a world of their own, but steadfastly refuse to be homogenized by someone else's.[11]

The beliefs and actions at the PoGC are an indigenous answer to existential anxieties experienced because of broken roots, poverty, and social and personal limitations. PoGC members get psychological and spiritual strength from the church's ritualistic performances, obtaining confidence on their own terms, in other words, in their pre-existing internal cultural substructures.

Religious beliefs become transformed or weakened with the changes in social relations after migrating from rural areas or when adjusting to constant urban changes – because people are forced to take a long look at the existing social and religious system. At first glance, the PoGC seems to be in the front line of changing people's lives and culture, but more careful examination reveals that sometimes the opposite is true. By choosing the PoGC, people would appear to be accepting its system, which not only represents social conditions and life patterns, but also the existing indigenous Aimaran identity.

The diverse approaches within the selected interviewees – new and old converts, youth and adults, urban and rural-born, ordinary members and intermediate leaders, male and female – show that they are all involved in the PoGC scenario in an openly cooperative fashion that masks an indigenous system that exists over and above the church structures. Conflicts, often unconscious, incongruous, and autonomous, occur in the conventional logic systems that actively guide people's actions. The standard logic is centred on rational thought, on measured common sense, on arguments based on what is good and what is bad. But the indigenous native system prevails, disqualifying rationality, and focusing on feelings and the spirit.

The cultural Aimaran vitality is also observable in inward manifestations through the perception of personal conversion, and concepts and experience

---

11. Knighton, *The vitality of Karamojong religion*, 261.

of mission, especially of evangelism and discipleship, and also in the opinions about integral mission held by ordinary members and intermediate leaders.

Conversion brings these people a flexible fusion of old and new perceptions, producing an identity formatted by indigenous ethnicity that is not entirely new. For the young, the change of heart sentimentalizes their perception; their conversion is focused on feelings. For adults, the transformation has more to do with moral values that are shaped by the native worldview.

Within Neo-Pentecostal belief, mission is an unavoidable duty. This is a mission exclusively focused on "winning souls." The responsibility of sharing and spreading this particular way of living the Christian faith is understood to be the major purpose of life. All the interviewees expressed this emphasis on spiritual matters, with spiritual needs as a priority, and material needs as secondary. Mission, therefore, is detached from the socio-political-economic context.

New believers adopt the gospel of Jesus Christ with an intense commitment combined with an attitude that is unselective about people and places. It is not important for them to share their testimony with relatives; they have a wider openness to a range of people and forms of influence. Older PoGC believers, on the other hand, strategically persevere with their extended family and friends. All of them practise their Aimaran communality when evangelizing or multiplying disciples. Intermediate leaders proselytize more willingly just to introduce people to the new faith. Pastor Guachalla, as principal leader, has a distinctive role of initiating others into the Christian faith in a way that mirrors many of the features of the traditional yatiri.

The global system exerts its uncontrollable power within Neo-Pentecostals at the PoGC – shaping their identity on the one hand while also reaffirming the Aimaran legacy. Obvious Westernized features can be observed but within the framework of traditional indigenous customs. Western Europe, Africa, and Asia have responded to the homogenization of humankind and democracy by splitting into more officially recognized countries. Never before has history seen as many national divisions as in contemporary times. The parable of the seed and the plant pot, the incarnational paradigm or the principle of acceptance and separation that the Apostle Paul applied, has been taken on board by Pentecostals. This is not a response to a rational understanding of the Bible, but a consequence of their own indigenous nature.

5

Aimaran Identity in the Power of God Church

Social Identity

The Aimaras who attend the PoGC embarked on a spiritual quest to respond to the disruption experienced in their lifestyle when they immigrated into continued poverty in La Paz. They looked for Neo-Pentecostal spiritual assistance congruent with the vital religious aspect of their indigenous cultural background.

For the Aimara, the dynamic life force comes from within, from the innermost soul which cannot be seen, but is as real and even more powerful than what can be seen. The Aimaran cultural identity is animist because the Aimara believes that the cosmos – with its indivisible wholeness and history – possesses spirit, soul, and life-giving strength. It is not only men and women who have spirit; for Aimara, the whole Universe is related and lives together.

There is no doubt that structural factors such as social, political, economic, and cultural considerations have affected the Aimaras' decision to adopt a Neo-Pentecostal identity; but, at an individual level, spiritual forces have also been involved. The interaction between structural and individual elements has transformed Aimaran identity from a dubious Aimaraized Catholic religiosity to active Neo-Pentecostalism. With the PoGC members, both individual and social identity processes are at work. The decision to assume Neo-Pentecostalism is related to macro structures that affect their daily life. Institutional social actors offered them a new public identity so they have moulded their personal Aimaran identity to fit the proposed Neo-Pentecostal identity – integrating autonomy as individuals with restraint from social configuration. As will be seen in this chapter in the analysis of primary resources, their understanding of their new situation is a blend of structural factors, in general, and the local indigenous contexts – both are involved in their construction of identity.

For Aimara people born in the city, the most intense conversion modifications occur within six months because life and circumstances change more quickly in the urban areas. For those who were born in the country and have lived in the city for at least five years, the change takes much longer because socio-religious mutations meet more resistance. At first sight, research indicates that after the initial phase of conversion to Neo-Pentecostalism, Aimaran Neo-Pentecostals experience another mutation in which they partially return to the worldview held before conversion. The grass roots study indicated that this return usually happens two years or more after conversion. Some of the findings from the focus groups are that different expressions of identity parallel with autochthonous popular religion (that is, new religious structures often combine Neo-Pentecostal experience with Aimaran ethnicity) and that growing awareness of women's rights is changing relations between the countryside and the urban periphery or between the local and the global.

Understanding the religious identity of Aimaran Neo-Pentecostals requires an awareness of their religious practices. They have specific, conscious, and unconscious demonstrations of Aimaran culture in daily life, whether at work or in worship. These are seen in: the use of cultural values in evangelism and funds collection; the use of folklore, music, dance, and language; the deep-rooted indigenous beliefs reshaping the imported ones and vice versa; and the strategy of the church's work.

To speak about the Bolivian Aimaran identity today is to speak about the experience of a people who have been nominally Roman Catholic for five centuries. Although they incorporated Catholic Christian religious values into their worldview, they continued to be culturally Aimaran, and their own identity has become more defined and stronger in the centuries since the Europeans arrived. Neo-Pentecostalism has a catalysing impact on this ongoing process. What do the Aimaran Neo-Pentecostals think about themselves and about the world? How do they conceive the material and spiritual world? What new identity has the Neo-Pentecostal experience given them?

Everyday Practices and Relations in the Family

Family life is fundamental to human existence. Communities made up of families have been observed in various Aimara contexts to be: bulwarks of social, moral, and religious traditions; socially constituted loci of identity; and both defenders and facilitators of modern values and changes.

Ayllu

Aimaras have a definition of community ethnically expressed by the word, ayllu. This word implies a rural community with social and territorial unity characterized by reciprocity and solidarity; in other words, by the ability to combine individual, family, and communal needs in harmony and reciprocity with the natural environment. Urban settings reproduce unexpected Aimaran communal and family adaptations of cultural ties based on traditions, and lead to different kinship relations. The desire to belong to a specific Aimaran community continues to be strong, both in those who have migrated to the city and in those born there.

In early childhood, guided by parents and the community, Aimaras learn that every part of life has spiritual significance – belonging to a community is something sacred. Aimaran reciprocity and solidarity are the cornerstones of community life in rural areas. This means sharing land, food, and any material and non-material resources. In the rural areas with agriculture and craftwork these socio-cultural cornerstones are still firmly entrenched, well organized, and efficient – although sometimes excluding those who are not part of the ayllu, especially if they are not Aimara.

On immigrating to the city, the framework of the rural ayllu practice disintegrates, but the ayllu is rebuilt and restored creatively and powerfully in an urban form. A question that needs to be answered is: Are Aimara immigrants creating an urban version of the ayllu which was originally rural? Is the church an extension of the ayllu?

The rural ayllu encompasses religious life, for each aspect of life has spiritual implications. While this spiritual meaning has been relocated to the urban setting, the relocation also presents an opportunity to construct new practices with similar meaning. The compartmentalized, divided, and detachable Westernized world-and-life view is not, after all, the understanding of the Aimaras. Very much like the first-generation Christians in the first century AD, their experience of life is integrated and holistic. For many Aimaras, the work of Neo-Pentecostalism is filling a religious and social gap. The PoGC teaches urbanized immigrant Aimaras to live in a new environment with an indigenous personality.

Gender Relations

After conversion, urban or urbanized married Aimara women continue to be homemakers with an average family of four children. Discriminatory attitudes against the female gender are common inside the home. However, in recent decades, significant changes have occurred showing more symmetry in the man-woman relationship. The traditional authoritarian role of the males is maintained but diminished, while the women have achieved more autonomy with the increasing participation of males in domestic tasks, such as cleaning, cooking, education, and childcare. At home, however, education and healthcare, especially children's health, are still more the mother's responsibility. The testimony of two rural-born women from the PoGC is "My husband helps me to cook, to wash, and rinse the clothes" and "We both help each another, on alternate days, except in the case of an emergency."

Husband-wife roles are more open and interchangeable in a contemporary Neo-Pentecostal home although these signs of "democracy" sometimes conceal an accepted chauvinism. Male hierarchy, however, is being questioned and subtly transformed. The way in which couples make important decisions shows an increasing balance in relationships. An Aimaran male born in the city said, "Since living with my wife, I don't like to say that certain domestic tasks are just for women, I am not a chauvinist. I talk with my wife and we do everything together." Such sharing of domestic duties is not always part of Aimaran collective imagery. However, the unbalanced rights and duties in family relations that are nourished by friendship and Aimaran ceremonial kinship seem to be more horizontal in the context of the PoGC members.

In poor countries like Bolivia, families with insufficient financial resources depend very much on the extended family. Parents, together with brothers, sisters, uncles, and grandparents work to face life's difficulties by combining their efforts in ways not possible for nuclear families. For food, work, health, and now for the purposes of Neo-Pentecostalism, extended families reinforce kinship links.

However, Neo-Pentecostals do not wait to leave home before becoming financially independent. The teaching and socialization within the church means that they rapidly adopt more individualistic behaviour and, as a result, small nuclear families are formed. Home has become a nucleus that is increasingly physically and economically independent of the extended family, although strong links are maintained between children, parents, grandparents, grandchildren, and uncles and aunts.

The parent-child relationship tends to transmit moderate patriarchal patterns. Parents, both fathers and mothers, teach their daughters domestic skills and their daughters' academic-professional aspirations are modest or carefully guided. Sons, on the other hand, are educated to play important roles in the religious, social, and economic world. Some parents expressed a desire for their sons to become pastors or church workers. This family patriarchalism is nurtured within the church via its organizational and ceremonial structures and also by the Bolivian society in general. In this aspect, the church appears to fill the vacuum in the lives of the younger generations left by the decision to distance themselves from the extended family.

Sirwiñacu

As noted in Chapter 2, the Aimara rural people have a marriage custom called sirwiñacu, which is a Quechua–Spanish word meaning mutual service. This word also expresses a pre-colonial belief that, for a marriage to work well, it needs a trial period before the official marriage ceremony is attended by the couple, relatives, and community members in general. Before the "official" wedding, the couple has an experimental time of living together, usually for about a year, and they remain faithful to each other before and after marriage. Through the centuries, sirwiñacu has functioned as a successful form of social control, making the family the foundation of the community and keeping the divorce rate for Aimaran marriages at less than 1 percent in rural areas. This, however, is not the case in cities like La Paz where conventions do not follow the same social patterns or exert the same pressure and social control. Nevertheless, urban Aimaran have adapted sirwiñacu and some members of the PoGC accept this practice.

Whereas traditional evangelicals radically reject sirwiñacu, Neo-Pentecostals are adapting it to their new urbanized identity. Expectations for the future change fast when poor, agricultural, rural life is replaced with a Westernized mind-set focusing on formal education and industrial facilities.

Education

The PoGC, within a context of poverty and governmental education policies, has transmitted the goal of studying at university to its Neo-Pentecostal families. Foreign-shaped values are also imposed by the experience of being raised in situations of extreme poverty.

An Aimara's future depends on being educated and becoming a "graduate-professional." Their future goals reflect Aimaran values and the modernized trends in urban people groups more than the teachings of the gospel. It seems that for Aimaran members, the PoGC is a bridge between a rural, animistic way of life and a Westernized, individualistic, urban worldview. Education for their children, especially at university level, represents the highest aspiration for most families.

Hard Work

The Aimara's dedication to work, albeit at subsistence level, is also found in members of the PoGC. Every day, including weekends, most of the workshop participants, including some of the women, begin work as street sellers early in the morning around 5:00 a.m., and go to bed around midnight. Working women also manage to get all the domestic chores done at home. With a few exceptions, PoGC members work in tough exploitative conditions within the informal economy. Wives and husbands – and often the children as well – work for very low returns.

Godfathers

Weddings, baptisms, and house removals are occasions for ceremonial kinship. Aimaran godparents, not necessarily relatives, are selected to share special dates, initiation ceremonies, and rites of passage. The social structure, as well as the education of new generations, is founded on this type of relationship. The complete series of social events and ceremonies provides the couple with all they need to set themselves up in family life and go through all life's stages with a sense of belonging. It also means they have moral duties to be fulfilled and enough social obligations to their relatives, *compadres* or godparents, neighbours, and friends to keep them busy for the rest of their lives.

Aimaran Neo-Pentecostals have changed the meaning of ceremonial kinship but not its practice. Some of them give new names to old relationships so they have "witnesses" rather than "godparents" to accompany them on special occasions like baptisms. The practice, however, remains and is reinforced by belonging to the same faith and church.

Continuity and change coexist in the context of the whole culture; they interact in the nuclear and extended family, ceremonial kinship, the community of faith, and society in which these Neo-Pentecostal evangelicals are immersed in constantly. In the daily routine, modern trends are expressed in different spheres of life and, as a result, transformations, adaptations, and changes take place.

Participation in Civic Organizations

Women believers from the PoGC, because of their work in busy open market areas with much sitting on the ground to sell their wares, participate actively in civic organizations, trade unions, and women clubs or neighbourhood organizations. New male believers tend to be more suspicious or apathetic about public affairs and political participation, at least at first. After the initial post-conversion period, PoGC adult members become more active in civilian-political organizations and union groups. The women join the trade unions associated with street sellers, craft workers, and food suppliers while the men participate in neighbourhood and union organizations linked with their area of work or ethnic-family tradition. Men usually lead these civil society organizations although this is flexible. Many organizations are happy to accept Christians in leadership positions, especially if handling money is involved, because it is widely believed that evangelicals have stopped lying and stealing and, therefore, are trustworthy.

In many cultures, men and women have different, complementary roles that bring natural social consequences. In Aimaran culture, women appear to be assigned administrative-domestic roles while men operate in the political-legal spheres; without tacit support for this gender distinction, conflict or indifference would occur towards the complementary gender group. Women's domestic, administrative, and employment-related activities prepare the way for men's political participation. The man's role also complements and affirms a woman in her tasks. Nevertheless, both women and men keep and develop a fundamental Aimaran relational value: the community life. This is put into practice in grassroots organizations that spontaneously arise in poor districts for survival purposes.

Today, Aimaras affected by the impact of Neo-Pentecostalism are convinced of the need to participate actively in civic organizations, bearing witness to their faith. On the issue of civic involvement, men sometimes have a different religious and more critical view. Here again there is a noticeable difference in attitude between old and new converts. After a period of isolation, Neo-Pentecostal Christians tend to return to civilian society organizations, although not to political parties as such. Political parties as a trustworthy form of citizen representation have lost credibility in Bolivia and not only among evangelicals, but also among others who have opted to give them a wide berth.

Social protest measures, like marches, roadblocks, hunger strikes, and human walls to lay siege on entities or entire cities – all of which have become commonplace in this part of the world – are far more effective people's participation processes for pressuring the government to meet social demands. Evangelical Neo-Pentecostal participation in politics and contemporary forms of social protest is an area for further study. Although evangelical Christians have made an important contribution to the indigenous movement's leadership since the 1950s, playing an active role and serving the social and political needs of the majority in the country, new evangelicals seem to have taken a step backwards.

Civic organizations function as a way of finding or generating jobs, linking citizens and corporate and cooperative employment initiatives, and improving public services and structures. At least once a year, civic organizations are distribution channels for food donated by charity or governmental institutions, perhaps for Christmas or another local event. Creating and balancing social intervention for survival meets communal and individual needs. Internal community values and structures are adapted and maintained through the support of grassroots organizations. Trade unions, mother's clubs, and different kinds of associations (whether employee, worklessness or neighbourhood based) seem to be fundamentally Western products of twentieth century modernity; but, for urbanized Aimaras, they replace authentic ethnic values and social needs.

The notion of native Neo-Pentecostals exchanging and stigmatizing ethnic religious identity is our own biased misunderstanding. The PoGC itself is a space for indigenous people to achieve new social structures – effectively appropriated and reinvented for their own needs and purposes. Native Aimaras subvert their new religious condition for their own purposes and find ways of resisting the imported paradigms. What is, then, the new Aimaran Neo-Pentecostal identity? Why and how are they reinforcing old roots and growing new ones? Are they combining two substantial contradictory forces? Are they organizing their own transformation which is now being impacted by the Neo-Pentecostal gospel?

Positive and relevant syncretism not only applies to the religious field (as commonly understood); it is also generic to the whole culture, as is seen in the case of Aimaran civic organizations. Again, it is important to remember that asserting the detachment of culture is reductionistic thinking and a misunderstanding. Aimaras neither conceive of existence nor behave in this way. In other words, for them, cultural identity is something holistic, integrated, a living system. Therefore, it needs to be explained in terms of theories that deal explicitly with wholeness. Ethnic religious identity is commonly treated as machinery that can be deconstructed or built piece by piece. That is not the case for the Aimaras. It is not possible to understand the complexity and richness of their ethnicity without paying attention to its interconnectedness with the whole world.

Coping with Crisis Situations

In crisis situations (sickness, death, unemployment, alcoholism) Neo-Pentecostals maintain their traditional Aimaran worldview, although this is weakening. Urban life acts as a temporary destabilizing factor for indigenous roots, even before the church gets involved. The PoGC deeply affects these aspects that are already relatively undermined, but without conscious rejection of the Aimara past, with its values and beliefs. However, new adaptations in religious identity in a context like the Neo-Pentecostal Aimaran context may underscore the assertion of identity.

This section provides a detailed description and analysis of how, in their statements, the workshop participants unanimously affirmed their rejection of traditional beliefs about the return of the soul after death, at least in principle. Nevertheless, many gave examples about how they bury the dead, observe All Souls' Day, confront terminal illness, and how they practise mourning. A ritualistic animistic worldview is preserved because an animistic relationship continues with those who have died. Death is an experience lived with considerable religious intensity because of the conviction that supernatural forces are operating over human beings.

In situations of terminal illness, Aimaran Christians' first resource is prayer, followed by medical doctors and modern medicines, after which some of them consult the Aimara religious and medical specialists (the yatiris). They believe that their dead relatives' spirits are loose everywhere and can appear at any time. After death they become living inhabitants of the invisible world, which is still very real and meaningful. This belief is rooted in the concept of the spiritual life adapted by Neo-Pentecostals. For example, instead of the Catholic nine-day mass for the dead, they hold a vigil or fast for the same period of time, that is for nine (or sometimes for seven) days after the burial. The belief that the spirits of ancestors walk, appear, and have power to make people sick or cry, is contradictory to what Christian Neo-Pentecostals have been teaching.

Christian grieving or mourning processes should be marked by thanksgiving and hope. Aimaras have a fatalistic approach to death – full of fear, sorrow, and uncertainty. The reinvented Neo-Pentecostal death rituals allow room for sorrow and broken heartedness in their all-night vigils. At public mourning ceremonies, like funeral services, processions, and burials, behaviour is obviously more socially controlled; but, in individual private arenas the belief in souls, with its deep-seated shared understanding of life, is more resistant to new alternatives. Traditional beliefs remain. The indigenous worldview persists with some minor alterations, but the foundation continues to be Aimaran. Christianity gradually transforms aspects and behaviours of these life-shaping perceptions but the fundamental identity continues to be Aimaran.

Some would say that the unifying forces of Aimaran ethnicity become negative when their collective practices involve alcoholism. Among rural Andean Aimara alcohol consumption always occurs within a social context. People do not drink alone. This situation changes, however, within the urban context where men and women do start to drink alone.

Some men and woman see alcohol consumption as something necessary believing that getting drunk together as a community group ensures employment. Although women and their children are frequent victims of physical and emotional violence, they maintain a passive attitude to alcohol. In these situations, Neo-Pentecostalism plays a role in encouraging perseverance and a faith-centred life. For others, violence is associated with ancestral heritage. Aimaras maintain a deep regard for ancestral heritage whatever the religious changes occurring towards the Catholic or Neo-Pentecostal faith and whatever the patterns of behaviour adopted by their ancestors. They certainly believe that curses and bad behaviour are part of the heritage received from previous generations.

One important Neo-Pentecostal paradigm is what they see as free access to the anointing of the Holy Spirit. The power of the Spirit of God, as they see it, is equally accessible and available to every believer. There is no need for mediation and every believer can be healed and experience victory over Satan. New birth into the Neo-Pentecostal faith is accompanied by the conviction that believers are the chosen ones who also receive the Holy Spirit. This comes with self-empowerment and the empowerment to perform miracles, particularly healing miracles. Everybody – not just the specialists – has access to spiritual power. Pentecostal pastors in the religious Aimaran context take advantage of special mediation powers after being empowered by supernatural forces. However, the PoGC members no longer expect the mediation of religious leaders for healing and spiritual warfare. The power of the Holy Spirit is given to each convert and entry into God's powerful presence is freely accessible to all.

Why do so many people convert to the Neo-Pentecostal gospel? What is it that attracts the Aimaran people to the PoGC? The reasons are not intellectual in nature. It is not a response to the search for sound doctrine or to fill a faith vacuum or to counter spiritual ignorance. Crisis situations play an important role in introducing people to the gospel; circumstances that produce suffering lead to seeking Neo-Pentecostalism. The response Aimaras find in the midst of scenarios of extreme suffering will determine whether the church will endure or not. In the Aimaran culture, it is extremely important to face life's crises holding onto a belief in the integral harmony of the cosmos throughout the circle of life: birth, rutuchi, military service, marriage, old age, death. The harmony of the cosmos includes the crises of ill health, malnutrition, and agricultural crises related to the sowing and harvesting seasons, such as drought and floods. In all of these situations, the key person in the community is the religious agent, the yatiri.

In the urban context, three new crises are added to this list. These are crises for which traditional Aimaran rituals have no answers: the crisis of alcoholism, the crisis of domestic violence (in which the woman is typically the victim), and the crisis of extreme urban poverty that comes with unemployment and low income. As a result, many people convert to Neo-Pentecostalism to resolve these non-traditional Aimaran crises. The PoGC rituals address the crises of alcoholism, domestic violence, and unemployment as sicknesses that are the fruit of sin or demon possession: the church prays for and anoints the sick; the believers pray against alcoholism; they make covenants of prosperity; and they cast out demons.

In extreme life or death situations where there is terminal illness or the presence of evil, the Aimara worldview influences Neo-Pentecostal experience. Dynamic and creative new dimensions are generated when coping with crisis situations and the Neo-Pentecostal identity is reshaped. The Neo-Pentecostal believer may think that only spiritual forces are in play, but several other factors such as education, poverty, language, and unemployment are involved in the situation. In the PoGC, diverse symbols are fit together to build a coherent religious identity system – the multiple meanings of many symbols are used simultaneously (such as the belief in the return of souls) and heterogeneous experiences are integrated through unifying symbols (such as the use of oil that has been blessed).

Aimaran Religious Actors, Rituals, and Festivals

In the Aimaran worldview, access to divinities must occur via specialists who are exclusive intermediaries. In the PoGC, however, the divine is accessible in a personal and direct manner. Nevertheless, there is a kind of fetishist spiritual mediation by the leader, especially in the use of oil which has been blessed by him for anointing the sick. This does not imply, however, a dominant form of intermediation. Freedom is allowed for individual creativity; action and initiatives are encouraged.

Older Neo-Pentecostal converts tend to gradually return not only to their Aimaran symbolic perception of life but also to practising some of the Aimaran rituals. Beliefs and rituals seem to persist and be practised; the old and the new sharing and contrasting some of their features.

The religious Aimaran main performer takes an active part in the celebration of special public holidays and saints' days. The PoGC's Protestant Neo-Pentecostals publicly reject (in theory) pagan patronage festivals because they consider them idolatrous and because they are always associated with drunkenness. However, at ground level, when festivals are organized in their workspace or in the streets, Aimaran beliefs, emotions, and intentions can come to light.

This partial Neo-Pentecostal rejection of paganism provides PoGC members with new opportunities to make closer relationships within the family and be more productive and dedicated to work. This, in turn, improves the quality of ties within the nuclear family and, consequently, their welfare.

Time and finances formerly invested in patronage festivals are redirected towards family needs and work. Money is no longer spent on alcoholic drinks, festival costumes, or the fees required to earn the right to participate in one of the folkloric-group associations. Neo-Pentecostal converts tend to participate less and less frequently in symbolic animistic-Catholic expressions of cultural and religious identity and this, in turn, can break up former bonding mechanisms with possible negative consequences. However, all dimensions of remodelling identity are redirected to reformulate and remould values, beliefs, and behaviour. Adaptations and changes, and continuity and discontinuity, arise as a spontaneous strategy for simultaneously rejecting and accepting symbols. It is impossible to see the interventions mentioned above as an utter rupture with pagan links – as expounded by evangelical preaching – but, at the same time, there is no complete continuity with traditional customs.

These Andean festivals reinforce community links via collective access to divinity. As a result, argue Neo-Pentecostal Aimaras, Aimaran identity is renewed. In these fiestas, economic surplus is exchanged for social prestige inasmuch as the *padrinos* (godparents) finance the party in exchange for social recognition and promotion in the social pecking order. The patronage festival legitimises the accumulation of wealth without making any ethical judgements. Socio-economic stratification processes occur with unquestioned religious absolution. The poor majority who participate in the fiesta respond passively to the abusive superiority demonstrated by the wealthy.

The active role of poor Neo-Pentecostals, encouraged by churches like the PoGC, in both religious and social fields becomes a type of "social re-vindication" that compensates for the discrimination the Aimaras suffer in collective scenarios such as patronage festivals. The PoGC has introduced functional substitutes for Aimara rituality as expressed in patronage festivals. Examples of this are: the party atmosphere of the church services; the opening and closing aspects of services which last for three hours, with worship songs that reflect the popular Aimaran style of music; the bands, now as essential in church services as they are in pagan festivals, playing songs with national and Latin rhythms.

For non-Neo-Pentecostals, these rituals work as key elements for self-determination, social engagement, and religious cultural continuity, but what do they mean for "born again" PoGC Neo-Pentecostal members? Are they innovating alternative forms of self-affirmation, determination of social identity, and spiritual reformation?

The variety of rituals for worshipping Pachamama, in particular, strengthens family ties. Kinship and community relationships are vital, overriding ethnic, social, and economic differences. Nevertheless, Neo-Pentecostalism challenges the continuity of traditional Aimaran identity without eliminating essential roots and links with a former worldview. The PoGC proposal would appear to offer a new commitment that breaks up the traditional status quo and promotes symbolic inversions of beliefs and behaviour. In other words, the comprehensive acceptance of shoulder-to-shoulder coexistence of new faith and resistance to the old worldview means that any identity analysis must be more flexible and realistic. Is it possible to view evangelical Neo-Pentecostal identity not as a religious expression that excludes Aimara cultural expressions but as something complementary? Are they essentially contradictory or is the ground being prepared to dynamically interact and create a new identity?

Just as the Jewish culture developed throughout the Old Testament period (before being subjugated to the globalizing Roman Empire) was the substructure for the primitive Christianity founded by Jesus and his disciples, so too the Aimaran religious worldview developed during the pre-colonial, colonial, and republican periods is the substructure for PoGC's Neo-Pentecostal Christianity within contemporary globalization. In other words, there are no cultural, historic, or religious vacuums into which the seed of the gospel of Jesus Christ can be planted. In the Andean side of Bolivia, the message is sown in indigenous soil, germinating, and producing fruit with flavours, colours, and shapes that are born out of its context. Neither Catholicism nor Protestantism with all their adaptations, including the Neo-Pentecostal version, have been able to remain immune to the deeply rooted structure of indigenous religious perception.

Maintaining Links with Ancestors and Rural Life

The forms of mutual help and collective work, common in rural Aimaran culture, are still very much alive among the faithful PoGC churchgoers. The growing impact of modernization processes, however, means that these practices are expressed in different ways that may seem contrary to, and distinct from, traditional Aimaran practices. Aimaran values, however, have lived through similar collision processes, some perhaps even stronger than today's modernity, and have found ways of adapting to new circumstances without self-destructing. The Aimaran custom of reciprocity, for example, stretches across all levels of relationships, from the work environment to decision-making at home, and is still an essential feature today. Reciprocity is the fundamental base for establishing social relations and is expressed via strong dynamic social mechanisms still practised by the nuclear family, rural relatives, and church brothers and sisters.

One new dimension in Aimara city-dwellers' relationship with their ancestors and rural communities is their involvement in missionary work. This type of activity has several distinctive aspects: the use of the Aimara language to share their faith, the return to familiar rural geographical places, and at least some personal links with relatives and Aimara Christians. These testimonies reveal that, on visiting their – or their parents' – rural communities, Aimaran missionaries communicate their Neo-Pentecostal faith and their urbanized lifestyle. This means that when rural relatives decide to relocate, they not only move to urban soil, but also into the church. This frequently implies a double adjustment – from country to city and from Roman Catholicism to Neo-Pentecostalism.

Native identity is strengthened when urban immigrants, both Neo-Pentecostals and non-Neo-Pentecostals, regularly visit rural Aimaran communities since these visits tend to renew or revive their essential ethnic values. The agrarian reform in 1953, despite its weaknesses and limited scope for indigenous peoples, mortally wounded the existing system of elitist ownership of large estates in the Altiplano. As a cultural, social, economic, and political strategy, the Aimaras, including some Neo-Pentecostals, maintain and encourage ties with relatives and property in rural areas.

Strategies of evangelism and work also accompany the constant interchange between countryside and city. Annual communal celebrations closely linked to the agricultural seasons are occasions to demonstrate freedom from alcohol, show some prosperity, and also to preach the gospel. Harvest and sowing ritual celebrations with native political and religious authorities and the symbolic distribution of crops play a significant role in identity and expansion challenges.

Most of the people who make the move from the country to the city do not achieve a total identification with urban life. First generation PoGC urban immigrants and previous generations born in the city all seem (in different degrees) to find balance with one foot in each world.

Rescuing the historical cultural memory in constant connectivity and relationality with the geographical place of birth, ancestors, grandparents, and parents revitalizes the worldview, enhances awareness about the importance of reaffirming indigenous ethnicity, and opens opportunities for service and growth.

Understanding Conversion

The mass conversion to Latin American and Bolivian Pentecostalism is a phenomenon that causes significant transformations in social and religious structural levels and also in the individual with immediate moral, spiritual, and identity consequences. People experience conversion every day. When those that are part of the PoGC speak of conversion, they do so with enthusiasm.

The evangelistic focus and personal commitment assumed in the PoGC (and which we observe in their services) motivates members to invite others, and even to insist upon attendance, especially with relatives and friends, with a view to achieving their conversion. This results directly in the exponential growth of the PoGC. Person-to-person sharing is a very important tool in Pentecostalism, even more effective than the mass media. The PoGC possesses and uses effective radio and television networks; however, these media do not supplant the place that personal contacts and oral communication have in traditional Aimaran ways for proselytising and conversion. Kinship, friendship, and relationships are important in conversion. Aimaran culture is essentially a culture of personal communication, in which men and women communicate orally.

Miracles are another important evangelistic tool. Healing is a vital part of the Neo-Pentecostal identity and tradition. PoGC members refer to this when retelling their conversion experience: "I became a Christian through my illness." "My son was sick, I wanted to kill myself if my son died, and in a blink of the eye my son was healthy again."

The topic of the miracles is criticized or viewed with scepticism, suspicion, or contempt by academic observers. However, for Neo-Pentecostals, starting from their conversion, it plays an important part in their identity and is reinforced by the certainty of God's supernatural action in the face of illness. The leaders, particularly the main pastor, are seen to be able to cure the body and the soul; but, in many cases, the ordinary members can also pray for miracles and see them happen. They believe that each one is a channel through which heavenly power flows.

There are subtle differences between the reasons men and women seek conversion, as it was observed in the focus groups. Women are motivated by family circumstances: problems with their husband, children, and/or in-laws; or insufficient income to cover food, school, and rent. Men, on the other hand, have more personal reasons: alcohol abuse, unemployment, and illness. One group seeks a new way of life because they are facing a family crisis, while the others look for an individual solution.

In essence, conversion is composed of changes; the concept is one of metamorphosis in which Neo-Pentecostals stop practising certain things. First and second-generation immigrants go through cultural and social adjustments that redefine their identity. Changes in the type and quality of work and housing redefine habits and introduce new ones. Concepts, language, and perceptions support the 'crashing in' of the new urbanized scenario that imposes modernization in a concentrated way. However, for Neo-Pentecostals from the PoGC, conversion adds another impact on their ethnic-religious identity with definitive moral consequences. This does not mean that their way of conceiving the Aimara world disappears, or that they block out their memory, or that they reconstruct a new identity from nothing.

Their conversion reconstructs spaces of change that are far more complex. They understand conversion as a breaking away from old practices, but this rupture is not handled in analytical terms with reason positioned as the axis. On the contrary, conversion is assumed in emotional and spiritual terms. It is emphatically not an option to use rational arguments to evaluate or criticize conversion. Aimaran members of the PoGC break their relationship with the past in principle, but what actually happens is that their past is remodelled. Conversion is a very personal decision that involves a key contemporary value – individuality. The life considered immoral by the church (alcoholism, idolatry, and parties) is left behind in order to embark on a new beginning. Although conversion has immediate consequences that change superficial structures, more deeply rooted structures often offer resistance and prove to be longer lasting. There may be significant changes in outward conduct, both at individual and group level, but the worldview remains solid. The mass conversions that occur quite frequently within the PoGC generate church policies of adaptation or accommodation thereby leading to paganism gaining a foothold within the Neo-Pentecostal church. The inclusive principle of the Aimaran logic system, without implying unlimited or uncontrolled inclusion, eliminates any impulse to live separated from the world, and blends conversion to a new faith with elements inherited from the existing indigenous sense of the universe.

Motivations and Interests in Attending the PoGC

The PoGC presents a deliberate absence in a participative articulation of its discourse and in the organizational structuring, this the work exclusive of the pastor, but at the same time the empowerment of its members is seen in practical areas. When they did not belong to the church, Aimaran members appealed to the yatiri as mediator. Now, the conversion has given them the confidence that they themselves are mediators between God and men. They are convinced that each one is a useful tool for the coming of the power of God to other people and for the expansion of the gospel by means of its proclamation. Now they can, without class or age distinction, heal the sick, announce the gospel, and cast out demons. This empowering makes the Aimaras feel that they are someone in society.

Every time they submerge themselves in at least one of the weekly services of the PoGC, they are "recharged" with the power and motivation to talk with friends and relatives about God. In each ritual ceremony there is a strong sense that desires and dreams are satisfied, that illnesses are healed, and emotional tensions are alleviated. They feel that their anxieties and fears are reduced – at least for the time that they are in the service for the church is a place where they feel at home. The church becomes an extension of the ayllu. The Neo-Pentecostal native Aimaras, who are different from second generation urban Aimaras, come to church with a trust, with a certainty, that they will not be defrauded and that they will not fail. The glossolalia, the electrifying ecstasies, the sacred laugh, are – in their renovated universe of beliefs – evidence that they possess the power of God and that they can pass on that power to others.

Community Atmosphere and Sense of Belonging

The people have several different reasons for attending church which tend to be mixed and complex, but I classify them in the following way. Firstly, people attend because of the community atmosphere they find; in other words, they seek a sense of belonging. But the testimonies are not all positive. Several interviewees complained about the size of the church, the lack of space, and feeling disappointed because the impersonal dealings raise barriers. It is difficult to be friendly or even recognize the people worshipping beside you in the PoGC because there are so many people attending, and they meet at so many different times over a period of years. It is a challenge to live a community life – ayllu – in the midst of growth in an already large church. The majority of participants in the seven workshops said that they have only a few friends in church. Nevertheless, the church is central in the life of its members and leaders maintain members are constantly enjoying a sense of belonging.

Empowerment

The second reason to be and to remain in church is an active participation and empowerment. The economically poor and the almost illiterate become rich and wise in spiritual terms. They possess and are possessed by the power of God to heal: they are convinced that the blessing of God is abundant over them. During the day, they are anonymous hard-working workers in the informal economy[1] sector, but in the church, they have the assurance that they are somebody. They are those who have been elected to participate in the advance of the kingdom of God. Because they are converted, they are empowered, they have access to the gifts of the Spirit, and they have enthusiasm and motivation for the expansion of their church.

Healing and Prosperity

Third, the attraction of being in the PoGC comes from an equation composed of two interdependent variables: healing and prosperity. To the question, "Why do you go to church?", the answers include, "To have a better life" and "For prosperity."

Undernourished people accustomed to suffering hunger, illness and poverty find satisfactory explanations and hope in the PoGC. They believe that they are or have been healed of their illnesses and that financial prosperity has already arrived although they do not see it yet. Cities or countries where Pentecostalism has grown and represents an appreciable percentage of the population are still growing in poverty and not in prosperity: no matter whether the global economy is booming or is in crisis, poverty in the last thirty years is increasingly *not* declining in Latin America and Africa. What passes at the macro level of society is a reflection of what is happening to families and individuals in Bolivia. Some Neo-Pentecostals progress or climb

---

1. The informal economy is a system of trade or economic exchange outside state control and not taxed by the government. It exists in Bolivian, Latin America, and countries worldwide.

up the social ladder, but many also remain in the same or worse conditions of poverty. However, they believe prosperity in capitalist terms is a promise from God. God fulfils his promise; therefore, the spiritually rich Neo-Pentecostal believes that he or she will also be economically rich and healed of all ailments.

Prayer and Ecstasy

The fourth attraction for PoGC believers is the experience of prayer and ecstasy. Repeated expressions during interviews described ecstasy as "fire that enters in the heart," "a heat that enters," speaking in tongues, strong shaking, always associated with practices of praying, and frequently occurring during the meetings of the congregation. The religious experience of each person is important and interesting. From the first Pentecost, believers have had access to the work and the gifts of the Holy Spirit. This charisma – manifested in speaking spiritual tongues, fire that burns, healings and trembling – is part of the Neo-Pentecostal experience and it exercises a powerful attractiveness on people. It becomes an essential element in the belief and practices associated with their new identity. It leads us to question whether the Aimaras from the PoGC, or any other Neo-Pentecostal church, are looking for salvation or seeking empowerment. Their desire to access power would explain their devotion, their prayer and fasting, the longing for ecstatic experiences, and speaking in tongues. They need salvation, but they also need enhanced self-esteem and empowerment. They want to obtain all three, but do they achieve what they hope via their understanding and commitment to the foundation of their faith and the gospel of Jesus Christ alone?

Another point worth evaluating is the ecstasy experienced within the church compared with the "'high'" found by drinking at Andean festivals. Chewing coca leaf and alcohol consumption are sacred for Andean peoples. Individuals consume coca as they go about their daily routines at work, at home, on public transport, etc. Alcohol, on the other hand, is normally reserved for social occasions, often at events associated with sacred rituals such as initiation and transition, or during a crisis when the ch'allado[2] is practised to honour the spirits. Alcohol is shared with the Andean gods and with other adults until people become so drunk that they experience a type of ecstasy. This leads us to ask if the ecstatic experiences offered in the PoGC fulfil a similar

---

2. *Ch'allar* means sprinkle in Aimara. The sprinkling is done to Andean spirits, especially to the Pachamama, as a sacred offering. It involves spilling or spraying some alcohol on the ground. Sagarnaga, Diccionario nativa Bolivia, 118.

function as the alcohol-induced ecstasy experienced at patronage festivals. Both experiences are inescapably linked to religious elements.

Practices of Piety

This church uses the verbal transmission of ideas very effectively. Pastor Guachalla is recognized as the main religious agent but no longer as the yatiri within Aimaran circles. The pastor has given all the church members the possibility and potential for transmitting action. They exhibit, however, a considerable dependence on the speech and ritual forms practised in the church. PoGC members repeat the forms of speech used by the leader by heart and attempt to imitate his lifestyle and practice of Neo-Pentecostal spirituality. The traditional spiritual disciplines of evangelical Protestants have changed in form and content in the PoGC. Prayer, healing miracles, and evangelism based on their personal experience replace the priority given to Bible study in other evangelical churches. Feelings are seen to be more important than rational thought.

Prayer

Prayer is by far the most common and disciplined practice of piety. Prayer permeates every aspect of life. If we compare the interview answers given by men with those of the women, the latter are clearly much more faithful and dedicated to prayer. The women pray in the church, at home, and in workplaces. They seek God's intervention through prayer. They speak to God to ask for the power of the Holy Spirit and to find a job. They intercede for good health and for the country.

Evangelism

The framework of Neo-Pentecostal piety where spirituality permeates every part of life also includes evangelism. It means sharing their faith with relatives and friends – but this involves talking more about their experience than the content of the gospel. They pray intensely for conversions. Their co-workers know that they have converted to Neo-Pentecostalism and, because of this, they speak about Jesus. They are simultaneously accepted and rejected in their new identity. On one hand, there are people who insist on speaking about God with them; but on the other hand, some fellow workers are people who curse believers and call them "witches." Their evangelism is motivated by a strong sense of urgency transmitted by the church, which preaches that the task must be completed and each believer must play his or her part.

The combination of praying, healing, evangelism, and exorcism is evident. All this is integrated, for example, in one visit to a sick person in the hospital. Women born in the rural area who have been in the church for more than two years (one of whom dresses in traditional, indigenous clothing) explained this using the Aimara language.

One woman said that, although she could not read the big Bible she was holding in her hands because she was illiterate, she carries that Bible everywhere with her. The Bible is her "partner, friend, and good luck."

Bible Reading

The woman quoted above was faithful to the evangelical tradition of always having a Bible in her hands; nevertheless, she could not read it. She gave a magic symbolism to the object – doing so is quite common in the PoGC. An important issue is raised here regarding the literacy levels within the PoGC and the relationship between the educational level of indigenous people living in the city of La Paz; the educational system and educational methodology; and, the importance of the Aimara language in the intellectual formation of urbanized natives and the magic symbolism of Neo-Pentecostal objects and rituals.

Traditionally, the reading of the Bible is an important mark of evangelical identity. Evangelicals are known as "the people of the Book." Non-Catholic Bolivian Christians have developed the habit of regular Bible reading and studying. This, however, is changing with Neo-Pentecostal evangelicals. The PoGC believers not only read their Bibles less frequently than Christians from more traditional denominations, but their capacity to study and understand the biblical text are weaker. The influencing factors are the low academic level of the indigenous people, the poor quality of the Bolivian educational system, and the Aimara's traditional orality. Literacy is an imported value; communication based on orality is an Aimaran value.

Innovating Piety Practices

Latin American Pentecostalism has not only changed the number of Protestants in Latin America, it has also changed their character. The conversion of Aimaras to Neo-Pentecostalism has implied the development of a new Christian spirituality, with old and new shades of Pentecostalism. At the same time that certain piety practices are abandoned, other new ones are introduced.

This is a process of constant change, which it is possible to observe in the PoGC services. There is an anxious search for innovations – to find new things that will capture people's attention. These new practices are then adopted into the church agenda and in the daily life of each member. The emphasis on prayer and the commitments to evangelism and to Bible reading are combined with fasting, visiting the sick, speaking in tongues, and the use of the PoGC mass media. These are basic and ongoing elements of Neo-Pentecostal spirituality. Other elements like the holy laugh, being slain in the Spirit, and exorcism come and go. They are secondary and transitory. All these expressions of their faith are moulded by the urbanized Aimaran worldview and constitute the religious Neo-Pentecostal being.

The forms of piety on which Neo-Pentecostalism rests are effectively disseminated inside the congregation starting with the careful selection of rituals and teaching practised by Pastor Luis Guachalla and his team. Tuning in and listening to Radio Sol also plays an important role in the spirituality of PoGC members, most of whom work in La Paz's open street markets, either sitting on the pavement or cramped into tiny shop spaces. Here they listen to the church's programmes: prayer meetings, healing services, fundraisers, and Pastor Guachalla's preaching. This is a small cameo of what happens throughout Bolivia where broadcasting plays an important communication and opinion-forming role in poor peri-urban districts and rural areas in which television and the internet have not yet made significant inroads.

Pastor Guachalla finds the working materials, inspiration, and tools for building his church's particular brand of piety in the experience of North American, Argentinean, and Brazilian Neo-Pentecostals. His preaching emphasizes the US version of prosperity theology, namely, "give more money offerings to God and he will multiply it and return it to you in the form of material goods and cash."

Nevertheless, the strong indigenous identity that permeates the church does not provide for replication of other models of ministry. The predominance and persistence of the Aimaran culture in the PoGC exercises a form of social control on the degree to which Western culture is allowed to influence the formation of the PoGC members' identity.

Perceptions Concerning Leadership

The great attraction of belonging to the PoGC congregation is the preaching and charisma of its pastor. Luis Guachalla, sixty-two years of age, is a former pastor of the most numerous and widespread evangelical group in Bolivia –

the traditional Pentecostal Assemblies of God. Compared to women, men tend to be more critical of the pastor's message and behaviour; although, at the same time, they uncritically repeat his ideas and words. They respect him as the maximum authority while seeing him as a fallible human being. Without doubt, he is their leader, the outstanding figure, the one with the capacity to communicate and make himself understood; not through concepts or academically methodical definitions, but through narratives – stories told often, including his own testimony. He has the ability to capture the hearts of people who, with dramatic emotion, point to him as loved, the father of all.

The evangelism practised at the PoGC under Luis Guachalla's leadership confirms and supports the validity of using the Aimara's mother tongue. The results of communication carried out in Spanish and then translated into Aimara are surprising. At the beginning, the church did not emphasize the importance of evangelizing in Aimara, but today it recognizes the effectiveness of the strategic use of the Aimara language. On this subject, Pastor Guachalla himself uses Aimara as much as possible given he is learning the language although, for the most part, he still depends on his translator. The leader's figure embodies the union of the old in the Bible and the modern Aimaran culture within a Westernized metropolitan city.

PoGC members usually carry a small bottle of blessed (or holy) oil in their wallet, handbag, or pocket in case it is needed to anoint the sick. This oil cannot be any kind of oil; it must have been blessed by Pastor Guachalla. The blessing is made every time the pastor prays to God for the oil. In this way, the leader enters into subtle territory where old Aimaran practices are transformed into something new. It is not only the sick who are anointed with oil to be freed from illnesses and become Christians – clothes, food, and merchandise are also anointed. Church members believe that when blessed fruits are placed on the table the person eating them will become a Christian. Food, clothes, and furniture have transforming power after coming into contact with the anointed oil. So, who heals? God or Pastor Guachalla? The common people of the congregation will unanimously affirm with strong conviction that it is God who heals.

The pastor's perception is that everyone understands that the power to heal and convert is supernatural and comes from God. However, people naturally do make a classification of those who are more able to heal, anoint, and convert; and, in this classification, Pastor Guachalla comes first, followed by his wife and their relatives.

Pastor Guachalla's communication skills contribute greatly to his congregation's remarkable growth. A flexible and vibrant scale of relationships has been established which speeds up exchange, service, and work. The church dynamics are centripetal – intense energy is focused on a central axis around which the movement rotates. This is the way it has always been and there is no sign of any plans to change this structure in the foreseeable future. Guachalla is very skilled and intelligent in discerning and handling the rapid social changes that leave Aimaran people who live in poor urban areas feeling empty and lost. He has learned how to catalyse these new paradigms and make use of them for the spiritual and missionary purposes of his work.

The PoGC, with its Westernized and globalized model, is penetrating and changing native Aimaran culture. However, it is tremendously challenging to get alongside the ordinary members of the congregation and learn about their plans, attitudes, and perceptions of themselves, the PoGC, and the world. What is the impact of the Aimaran culture in its Neo-Pentecostal experience? On observing and analysing the transformations that occur in the dynamics of the daily life, Aimaran identity in all its dimensions remains very active and influential in the Neo-Pentecostal identity. Aimaran beliefs, values, and customs are a significant part of the Neo-Pentecostal identity, as well as its theology and mission.

Conclusion

The Neo-Pentecostal church makes men and women progressively more autonomous in the areas of gender, extended family, and finances. They also become active participants in church activities. This creates an optimal situation for the expansion of this type of Christianity by giving people a strong sense of self-realization – because the individual convert now possesses the gifts of the Holy Spirit. Nevertheless, although most new converts temporarily reject their indigenous culture, at least in theory and sometimes by satirising many Aimaran beliefs, those who participated in the focus groups still maintain a living relationship with their native worldview. To describe the identity of Aimaran Neo-Pentecostals, this chapter has analyzed their daily life, family relationships, achievements, social links, and church membership. These multiple dimensions and collective tolerance of certain practices could also be called *intentional ambiguity*. Intentional ambiguity leads to a position that avoids an intolerant dualism between what has totally changed and what has not changed. There are aspects that have changed and others that have not changed; but where things have changed, the Aimaran identity is at work and vice versa. This is seen most clearly in the following aspects of life.

1. Neo-Pentecostal daily life and family relations
    - There is increased symmetry in Aimaran–Christian gender relationships despite wider evangelical and national chauvinism
    - Communal decision-making is based on consensus-building within nuclear families and extended kinship relationships
    - Poverty is faced with intentional tolerance; lifestyles that combine working hard in uncomfortable situations for twelve hours a day or more, completing domestic duties, and fulfilling church commitments are assumed with acceptance.
2. Participation in civic organizations
    - Contrary to what the leadership teaches about taking part in politics, older ordinary members of the PoGC play an active role in grassroots organizations thereby mirroring the rural ayllu in the urban context.
3. Coping with crisis situations
    - There is no sign of a conflict between the old and the new in the issue of the return of the soul after death. Church members affirm that they no longer hold on to this belief despite maintaining a belief in the continuity of their relationship with deceased ancestors.
4. Aimaran religious actors, festivals, and rituals
    - Neo-Pentecostals who have been converts for more than two years gradually return to Aimaran ethnic symbolism, rituals, and religious agents even though, according to the official voice of their church, they reject the paganism that these aspects represent.
5. Maintaining links with ancestors and rural life
    - Urban Aimaras' traditional values, language, social relationships, fiestas, and beliefs are nurtured, strengthened, and adapted through regular contact with rural communities.
6. Understanding of conversion
    - Significant individual and collective transformations do take place, and evangelism and healing both become part of life, but these variations do not occur in a void; they occur within the Aimaran worldview, which remains solid.

7. Motivations for church membership
   - Each Neo-Pentecostal believer is empowered to be a channel of divine power. Although motivations towards church membership can sometimes be individualistic (for example, the search for healing, ecstatic experiences, and prosperity), the overall motivation is experiencing an Aimara sense of community and religious life.
8. Practices of piety
   - When Neo-Pentecostal Aimara pray, heal, experience ecstasy, and cast out demons, it is possible to identify an implied holistic interrelationship between nature, human beings, and the cosmos – indigenous spirituality is being made manifest.
   - The Bible and the oil used for healing (after being blessed by the leader) have become assigned symbols of miraculous power.
9. Perceptions concerning leadership
   - Church members believe that clothes and food anointed with oil blessed by Pastor Guachalla can make changes in life and convert people; this is reminiscent of beliefs about the power and practices of the yatiri
   - Oral communication using narratives of popular stories is used wisely and in a widespread manner.
   - The Aimara language is still more expressive and effective than Spanish in communication at different levels of relationship.

Many languages and cultures are bi-dimensional; they dichotomize between absolutes such as spiritual versus non-spiritual and rational versus affective. Aimaras make absolutes into relatives because they always have a third (or more) alternative option in their multi-dimensional logic. This means they can be very tolerant and patient with new propositions – adapting them to their worldview without any sense of incongruity or conflict.

The Neo-Pentecostal PoGC is an example of the persistence of the Aimara's native religious worldview finding its own adaptations to, and symbiosis with, this form of Christianity. Something very similar occurred with the first Christians who were heirs of the indigenous Jewish conscience – their own particular indigenous consciousness. They did not want to change their religion but they did want to convert others to their newfound faith – a conversion that would take them from who and what they were culturally and religiously to what they wanted to believe and be in Christ – a process that ultimately transformed something that already existed into something that had not been seen previously.

Analysis and Findings

After a pertinent and holistic enquiry, this analysis and evaluation of the Power of God Church's Neo-Pentecostal identity demonstrates that the Aimara's Neo-Pentecostalism remains strongly Aimaran. The Aimara's indigenous roots and worldview permeate their new Christian identity.

When the gospel of Jesus Christ touches and penetrates the individuals within a community, wherever and whenever that may be, it works as a light with seen and unseen consequences. All things are transformed under Jesus's bright light and the darkness is increasingly defeated. The manifestation of Jesus in words or in deeds is not neutral or negligible.

The technological and industrial progress achieved by scientific and philosophical development and the uncontrolled use of natural resources by the creators and children of the Enlightenment – who are also the designers and heirs of modernity and, more recently, postmodernity – have generated an unprecedented moral and social collapse in humanity. The more highly urbanized societies are the most afflicting of others in this collapse, becoming the vanguard of the destruction of natural and human ecology as reflected in global warming, the disappearance of species, and the decay of the family as the backbone of society.

A widespread negative understanding of non-Western studies is no surprise since social sciences like anthropology are daughter disciplines of the Enlightenment with its long history of errors that supported racism against the blacks, the extermination of indigenous peoples, apartheid in South Africa, and many other similar cases – some of which affected indigenous peoples in Latin America. The natives of many lands have brought with them their own particular lifestyles and foci on spiritual life; these enrich global human experience and bring greater depth to other religions, including Christianity.

Aimaras in Latin America are no exception. Reports and studies from other parts of the world show how indigenous peoples are contributing forms and content that broaden and enrich integral perceptions of life. The trials and tribulations suffered by the Aimara during the centuries they lived under segregationist domination have not been in vain. The changes being experienced by the Aimara are typical of what is currently happening throughout the world. Growing global interdependence has opened the door for segregated human groups to become involved – although for many this is still seen to be a concession rather than a dialogue of equals. Through this slow-growing respect for constructive pluralism and syncretism, there is hope that human beings will become more fully human and perhaps even that Christians will become more fully Christian.

The Aimara have their own operating system and ways of representing their religion. For example, their rituals are not simply religious acts but expressions of social procedures, political realities, economic intentions, felt emotions, and physical movements. These features should be understood together as a complete package, a united whole that integrates the spirit and the mind and the soul in every part of life, and this is reflected in the loud and ostentatious mass meetings in the PoGC. Aimaran believers, on attending church, do not do so for reasons that are merely doctrinal, but also with holistic expectations and understanding. Conversion to Neo-Pentecostal faith, therefore, has a profound consequence on several aspects of daily life and family relationships while mirroring several deeply-rooted aspects of their cultural tradition. Church members participate in civic organizations which can be analogous to the traditional ayllu in rural areas. On facing crisis situations, indigenous urban dwellers may revert to Aimaran religious performances and performers, revealing the strength of old links with ancestors and rural life. Also, in their understanding of conversion, motivations for church membership, piety practices, and perceptions concerning leadership, there is no room for doubt – the church's solid, active platform clearly has an essentially Aimaran religious substructure.

Every religious or social Aimaran Neo-Pentecostal expression condenses, and potentially reveals, the cognitive, cultural, social, and extra-ritual processes of the groups practicing them. This book has tried to take a firm stand against the disintegrating, dehumanizing arguments of modern dichotomist rationalism by adopting two positions: first, by listening to the holistic perception and voice of ordinary Aimara Neo-Pentecostals and, second, by studying what national and foreign social scientists with long-standing, significant relationships and identification with Aimara and indigenous people in Latin America have to say in their research findings. It avoids any monocultural reading of this indigenous group from the Bolivian Altiplano using preconceptions of an external configuration. As a result, this study has concluded the influx of Aimara people into Neo-Pentecostalism has made them agents for integrating something into Christian experience that is impossible to separate or arrange hierarchically – the body from the spirit or space from time. What makes the Aimaran culture different is its vision of life as something complete and integrated, essentially spiritual, and in harmony with the cosmos.

The Neo-Pentecostal believer is someone who believes in the core doctrines of Christianity but who, like any other human being, can enact false beliefs or act in contradiction to the beliefs he or she holds dear. Religious rituals guide his or her existence in this world, but by no means hold the monopoly in this realm. Believing is not only, or emphatically, a mental occurrence or a mere psychological state. The complete existential condition does not include the prior assumption of a dominant hierarchy (found in intellectualism) in which reasoning comes first, and is followed by actions that respond to and reflect that reasoning. Different objects of belief can determine different possible responses.

For the Neo-Pentecostal believer, belief in divine healing does not rule out the use of scientific or natural medicine. Balance is achieved via the subtle combination of compatible and opposing elements, implying that the tripartite logic of the Aimara language and Aimaran worldview is at stake. The relativity of absolutes has outlasted the test of time and remains an important element of Aimara thinking and identity for Aimaras in general. The same is true for Aimaran Neo-Pentecostals. Just as Einstein's theory of relativity views rest and motion as being a relative dimension in relation to the speed of light, how and what people believe or do not believe are relative factors in relation to the whole indigenous cosmology. Whereas the bipolar Western logic creates interminable conflicts of opposites, the three-dimensional logic system tends towards the conciliation and coexistence of elements, some of which are contradictory. Good and evil live side by side; the future is the past and the past is the future in the present. The nutrient of indigenous tripartite logic is the relational cosmic system rooted in reciprocity and solidarity.

The beliefs practised by Aimaran Neo-Pentecostals do not start with a list of dogmas in a tightly defined creed that must be understood, nor is Aimaran Neo-Pentecostalism based on what individuals believe. If that were so, Neo-Pentecostalism would be entering the dangerous and partial terrain of submitting undecipherable mental events to the merely rational. The Aimara's neo-Pentecostal religiosity is based on visible ritual acts where people make a public commitment to adhere to their new faith within their own cultural tradition, acting in line with collective group representations.

The Aimara's Neo-Pentecostal faith, like most indigenous religions, has no explicit creed; it is composed of institutions and practices. The purpose of Aimaran beliefs and religious practices is not theological discussion or proselytization using rational arguments, but the survival and wellbeing of the community. The goal of Aimaras within the PoGC is not only to save souls but the survival and continuity of their community in the urban world.

Just like the Catholics who landed in Latin America with their Spanish form of Christianity, Pentecostals and evangelicals generally combine old and new, collective and individual, elements of salvation where everything rests on the foundation of an already-existing cosmology. Indigenous Aimaran rituals have an expressive and symbolic meaning. They symbolize: the shared feelings of group solidarity; appreciation for, and inevitable reference to, the past; and, a break with, and loyalty to, coactive tradition. Much of this has been inserted, adopted, and adapted in Neo-Pentecostal churches like the PoGC.

So why are Neo-Pentecostals so attractive? Instead of a structured, coherent system of ideas and thought, they issue a persuasive offer to experience God intensely. They offer a road to the solution for life's challenges – knowing and experiencing God himself. This experience of God involves no bureaucratic intermediaries and is communicated in familiar, easy-to-understand language by someone the listener can identify with – usually from the same people group and social class. The Neo-Pentecostal experience is even more attractive because it involves becoming part of a community of people who share the same experience and celebrate it warmly and enthusiastically with their new brothers and sisters in the faith.

The symbolic group context centres on the magic of the spoken word. If for the Aimaran people in general, their culture is a spoken relational culture, the Aimaran Neo-Pentecostal emphasizes its rituals via spoken relational aspects. Oral rather than written communication is important. Testimonies are appreciated more than preaching. Oral testimonies are crucial to the symbolic efficacy of Pastor Guachalla's dramatized sermons. The focus is on feelings rather than intellectual understanding. The pastor effusively and orally communicates narrative thought. Hence the vital importance of attending the PoGC church to hear the pastor's moving speeches delivered in a simple, intentionally narrative, orality. These speeches are not purposed primarily towards making and transmitting rational arguments, but towards communicating emotions and stirring feelings. The focus is on the *heart* rather than the mind. The spell cast by the pastor's words holds such strong power that some people never want to miss a church meeting and can be found in church every day of the week. The growing use of the Aimara language in the pastor's translated sermons and the unquestioned healing testimonies given by church members add to the emotional charge of the rituals practised in church services. An interpreter who translates sermons into Aimara does an excellent job of capturing exactly the dramatic tone used by Pastor Guachalla and the result is crucial for his listeners. The television programmes broadcast by the PoGC also reflect this effusion. The Aimaran emphasis on the oral narrative and the almost total absence of written material is also found in the church. The emotional symbolism of the oral word is one of the most anxiously awaited highpoints in the church service, especially when people are invited up to the platform to give testimony of recent miracles. The pastor interviews them, asking questions which gradually lead the interviewee and the congregation into a climax of ecstasy.

The Bible entails the principle of totality and is the visible symbol of salvation as a moral and behavioural code. However, Neo-Pentecostal discourse and practice are related – in the complex dynamic of continuity and discontinuity – with orality, with popular culture, and the indigenous religious-animist form of expression. As a result, Neo-Pentecostalism can espouse new religious feelings using an oral language and religious practices that evoke the indigenous world, are familiar to the people, and can be assimilated by them in a natural manner.

The Neo-Pentecostal experience in the La Paz Power of God Church is first and foremost Aimaran. Its core identity is defined by that culture's values, cosmic oneness, orality and linguistic equity, transcendental spirituality , and its three-dimensional logic system. All this and so much more form the character of the Aimara Neo-Pentecostals, what they are today, and what motivates them in their mission. It is worth making the observation that contemporary Neo-Pentecostal Aimara have a great deal in common with the first Old Testament believers and their history, people groups, and identity. There is also significant equivalence with New Testament Christianity: its cultures, people, and worldview.

The coming of Jesus Christ's gospel to an Aimaran context can be compared using the metaphor of the seed and a pot. The seed is the gospel, the seed goes everywhere. When the seed is sown in an African soil pot, the plant that comes out has an African identity. When the seed is sown in Latin America, the growing shoot has a Latin American innate look and personality. Believers and non-believers cannot control the incursion of light in the person and words of Jesus. The gospel is imprisoned by the soil pot but at the same time it is the liberator of culture.[3]

---

3. Walls, *The missionary movement in Christian history*, 3.

Bibliography

Albó, Xavier. "La experiencia religiosa Aymara." Pages 81-130 in *Rostros Indios de Dios*. eds. Manuel M. Marzal, Xavier Albó, Eugenio Maurer, Bartomeu Melia, and J. Ricardo Robles. Lima: Pontifica Universedad Catolica del Peru, 1991.

———. ed. Raices de America: El mundo Aymara. Madrid: Alianza Editorial, 1988

Albó, Xavier, and Matias Preiswerk. *Los senhores del Gran Poder*. La Paz: Centro de teologia popular, 1986.

Anderson, Allan. *An Introduction to Pentecostalism: Global Charismatic Christianity*. Cambridge: Cambridge University Press, 2004.

———. *Spreading Fires: The Missionary Nature of Early Pentecostalism*. London: SCM Press, 2007.

Arnold, Denise Y., and Alison Spedding. *Mujeres en los movimientos socials en Bolivia 2000–2003*. La Paz: CIDEM/ILCA, 2005.

Bastian, Jean-Pierre. *Protestantismos y modernidad latinoamericana: Historia de unas minorias religiosas activas en America Latina Mexico*. D.F.: Fondo de Cultura Economica, 1994.

Barrett, David y Johnson, Todd. *World Christian Trends, AD 30 – AD 2000*. Pasadena. Libreria Carey, 2003.

Beck, Robin. "Platforms of power: House, community, and social change in the formative Lake Titicaca basin" PhD Thesis, Evanston: Anthropology Northwestern University, 2004.

Bediako, Kwame. *Theology and Identity: The Impact of Culture upon Christian Thought in the Second Century and Modern Africa*. Oxford: Regnum Books, 1992.

———. *Christianity in Africa: The Renewal of a Non-Western Religion*. Edinburgh: Edinburgh University Press, 1995.

Berg, Mike, and Paul Pretiz. *Spontaneous Combustion: Grass-Roots Christianity, Latin American Style*. Pasadena: William Carey Library,1996.

Beyer P & Beaman L eds. *Religion Globalization and Culture*, Leiden: Brill, 2007.

Bosch, David Jacobus. *Transforming Mission: Paradigm Shifts in Theology of Mission*. New York: Orbis Books, 1991.

Bouysse-Cassagne, Therese. *La identidad Aymara: Aproximacion historica, siglos XV–XVI*. La Paz: Hisbol, 1987.

Bouysse-Cassagne, Thérèse, Olivia Harris, Tristan Platt, and Verónica Cereceda. *Tres reflexiones sobre el pensamiento andino*. La Paz: HISBOL, 1987.

Bowman, Charles H. *Vicente Pazos Kanki: Un Boliviano en la libertad de América*. La Paz: Editorial Los Amigos del Libro, 1975.

Buckingham, Jamie. *Daughter of destiny: Kathryn Kulhman...her story*, New Jersey: Logos International, 1976.

Canclini, Arnoldo. *Diego Thomson: Apóstol de la enseñanza y distribución de la Biblia en América Latina y España*. Buenos Aires: Asociación Sociedad Bíblica Argentina, 1987.

Cardenas, Victor Hugo. "La lucha de un pueblo" in *Raices de America: El mundo Aymara* ed. Xavier Albó. Madrid: Alianza Editorial, 1988

Carter, William E., and Mauricio Mamani. *Irpa Chico: Individuo y comunidad en la cultura Aymara*. La Paz: Editorial Juventud, 1982.

Chambers, Joseph. "Kathryn Kuhlman and her spirit guide." Available at http://www.pawcreek.org/kathryn-kuhlman/ Accessed 22.08.08

Cook, Guillermo ed. *New Face of the Church in Latin America: Between tradition and Change*. New York: Orbis Books, 1994.

Colque, Abraham "Identidad indigena, Nueva Constitucion Politica del Estado y desafios para la evangelización." Public Lecture given at the Fraternidad Teologica Latinoamericana, La Paz, 24 April 2008.

Comisión Conferencia Misioneros Bautistas en Bolivia. *El Cincuentenario de la Misión Bautista Canadiense en Bolivia: Desde su fundación en el ano 1898 hasta el principio del ano 1948* La Paz: Editora Universo, 1948.

Córdova Julio. "Tres ideas equivocadas sobre el movimiento neopentecostal" in *Fe y prosperidad: Reflexiones sobre la teologia de la prosperidad*, edited by Lourdes Cordero, 109-34. La Paz: Editorial Lampara, 1999.

Cox, Harvey. *Fire from Heaven: The Rise of Pentecostal Spirituality and the Reshaping of Religion in the Twenty-First Century*. London: Cassell, 1996.

Crespo, Alberto. *Alemanes en Bolivia*. La Paz: Los amigos del libro, 1978.

De Calderon, Eunice. *Porque el Señor así lo prometió: El avivamiento que conmovió a Bolivia*. La Paz: Producciones Anakainoo, 2004.

D'Epinay, Christian Lalive. *El refugio de las masas: Estudio sociologico del Protestantismo en Chile*. Santiago, Chile: Editorial El Pacifico, 1968.

Deiros, Pablo A. *Historia del Cristianismo en América Latina*. Buenos Aires: Fraternidad Teologica Latinoamericana, 1992.

Dempster, Murray W., Byron D. Klaus, and Douglas Petersen eds. *The Globalization of Pentecostalism: A Religion Made To Travel*. Oxford: Regnum Books, 1999.

Diaz Cruz, Rodrigo. *Archipealago de rituales: Teorías antropológicas del ritual*. México: Antrophos Editorial, 1998.

Droogers, André, "Visiones paradójicas sobre una religión paradójica. Modelos explicativos del crecimiento del pentecostalismo en Brasil y Chile", in Barbara Boudewijnse et al., *Algo más que opio. Una lectura antropológica del pentecostalismo latinoamericano y caribeño*. San José, DEI. 1991

Duncan, Robert. "Kathryn Kuhlman: healer and New Age diva." Accessed 23.08.08. Available at http://www.speroforum.com/site/article.asp?id=13001

Dussel, Enrique, Jeffrey Klaiber, Fernando Aliaga Rojas, Josep M. Barnadas, José Maria Vargas, Mortimer Arias, Catalina Romero, Cecilia Tovar, and Jorge Moreno

Alvarez. *Historia general de la iglesia en América Latina, VIII, Perú, Bolivia y Ecuador*. Salamanca: CEHILA, 1987.

Dussel, Enrique. ed. *The Church in Latin America 1492–1992*. New York: Orbis Books, 1992.

Eliade, Mircea. ed. *The Encyclopaedia of Religion: Phenomenology of Religion*. London: Macmillan, 1987.

Escobar, Samuel. "Que significa ser evangelico hoy?" *Revista Mision* 1:1 (1982): 6–9.

———. "Conflict of Interpretations of Popular Protestantism" in *New Face of the Church in Latin America: Between tradition and Change*, ed. Guillermo Cook, 112.34. New York: Orbis Books, 1994.

———. "The Promise and Precariousness of Latin American Protestantism" in *Coming of Age: Protestantism in Contemporary Latin America* ed. Daniel Miller, 3-35. Lanham, University Press of America, 1994.

Escobar, Samuel, Estuardo McIntosh, and Juan Inocencio. *Historia y mision: Revision y perspectivas*. Lima: Ediciones Presencia, 1994.

Estermann, Josef. *La filosofía andina como alteralidad que interpela: Una critica intercultural del androcentrismo y etnocentrismo occidental*. La Paz: ISEAT, 2004.

———. *Filosofia Andina: Sabiduria indigena para un mundo nuevo*. La Paz: ISEAT, 2006.

———. ed. *Teologia Andina: El tejido diverso de la fe indigena, tomo I y II*. La Paz: ISEAT, 2006.

Freston, Paul. "Pentecostalism in Latin America: Characteristics and Controversies" *Social Compass* 45 (1998): 335–58.

———. "Latin America: The 'Other Christendom', Pluralism and Globalization" in Beyer P & Beaman L eds. *Religion Globalization and Culture* eds. P Beyer and L Beaman, 571–94. Leiden: Brill, 2007.

Frias Mendoza, Víctor H. *Mistis y mokochinches: Mercado, evangélicos y política local en Calcha*. La Paz: editorial Mama Huaco, 2002.

García Canclini, Néstor. *La globalización Imaginada*, México DF: Editorial Piados, 1999.

Garrard-Burnet, Virginia. "Identity, Community and Religious Change Among the Maya of Chiapas and Guatemala." *Journal of Hispanic/Latino Theology* 6 (1998): 61–79.

Garrard-Burnett, Virginia, and D Stoll eds. *Rethinking Protestantism in Latin America*. Philadelphia: Temple University Press, 193.

Gospel and culture, Willowbank Report (Bermudas: Lausanne occasional paper 2, 1978).

Goytia Rodríguez, Jaime. *Principios de la obra Cristiana evangelica en Bolivia*. Cochabamba: Union Bautista Boliviana, 1993.

Guachalla, Luis. "Raices del ministerio del nuevo pacto Poder de Dios." Recorded message 9th November 2003. La Paz: Iglesia Poder de Dios, 2003.

Guaygua, German. "El mercado y los bienes de salvacion: consumo y habitus religioso en la zona del Gran Poder", MPhil thesis, Universidad de San Andrés department of Sociology, 1998.

Guaygua, German, and Beatriz Castillo. *Identidades y religión: fiesta, culto y ritual en la construccion de redes sociales en la ciudad de El Alto.* La Paz: ISEAT, 2008.

Hansen, Guillermo. ed. *El silbo ecumenico del Espiritu: Homenaje a José Míguez Bonino en sus 80 años.* Buenos Aires: ISEDET, 2002.

Hudspith, Margarita Allan. *Ripening Fruit: a History of the Bolivian Indian Mission.* New York: Harrington Press, 1958.

Jolicoeur, Luis. *El cristianismo Aymara: Inculturacion o culturización.* Cochabamba: Ediciones ABYA-YALA, 1996.

Klein, Herbert S. *Bolivia: The Evolution of a Multi-Ethnic Society.* New York: Oxford University Press, 1982.

Knighton, Ben. *The Vitality of Karamojong Religion: Dying Tradition or Living Faith?* Hants: Ashgate, 2005.

Lopez, Dario. *El nuevo rostro del pentecostalismo latinomericano.* Lima: Ediciones Puma, 2002.

———. *La fiesta del Espiritu: Espiritualidad y celebración pentecostal.* Lima: Ediciones Puma, 2006.

Lozada Pereira, Blithz. Identidad y vision del mundo Aymara, II Seminário Internacional del Pensamiento Andino, Cuenca: UNESCO. 2005

Llanque Chana, Domingo. *La cultura Aymara: Desestructuracion o afirmación de identidad.* Puno: IDEA, Instituto de Estudios Aymaras,1990.

Ma, Julie C. *When the Spirit Meets the Spirits: Pentecostal Ministry among the Kankanaey Tribe in the Philippines.* Frankfurt: Peter Lang, 2001.

Mackay, Juan A. *El Otro Cristo Español.* Mexico: Casa Unida de Publicaciones, 1952.

Mariategui, José Carlos. *Siete ensayos de interpretacion de la realidad peruana.* Lima: Amauta, 1976.

Martin, David. *Tongues of Fire: The Explosion of Protestantism in Latin America.* Oxford: Basil Blackwell, 1990.

———. *Pentecostalism: The World Their Parish.* Oxford: Blackwell, 2002.

Marzal, Manuel M. *El sincretismo iberoamericano: Un estudio comparativo sobre los Quechuas (Cusco), los Mayas (Chiapas) y los Africanos (Bahía).* Lima: Pontifica Universidad Católica del Perú, 1985.

———. *Tierra encantada: Tratado de antropología religiosa de América Latina.* Madrid: Editorial Trotta, 2002.

Marzal, Manuel M., Xavier Albó, Eugenio Maurer, Bartomeu Melia, and J. Ricardo Robles. *El rostro indio de Dios Lima*: Pontifica Universidad Catolica del Peru, 1991.

Mesa Gisbert, Carlos D., de Mesa Jose, and Gisbert Teresa. *Historia de Bolivia.* La Paz: Editorial Gisbert, 1997.

Mesa Gisbert, Carlos D. *Territorios de libertad.* La Paz: PAT, 1995.

Míguez Bonino, José. *Rostros del Protestantismo latinoamericano*. Buenos Aires: Nueva Creación, 1995.
Miller, Daniel ed. *Coming of Age: Protestantism in Contemporary Latin America* Lanham: University Press of America, 1994.
Ministerio del nuevo pacto Poder de Dios. *'Gran avivamiento de Bolivia a las naciones'* Available at http://www.poderdedios.com/ Accessed 2.10.08. 2008
Morrillo, Grace. *Critique of the transformations video*, 2004. Available at http://www.lam.org/news/article.php?id=371 Accessed 1.09.08
Murra, "El aymara libre de hoy" in *Raices de America: El mundo Aymara* ed. Xavier Albó. Madrid: Alianza Editorial, 1988
Nacho, Arturo. "Historia de la obra Bautista en Bolivia: Un enfoque misiologico al aproximarse a su centenario." MPhil Thesis, Seminario Teológico Bautista, 1994.
Naugle, David K. *Worldview: The History of a Concept*. Grand Rapids: Eerdmans, 2002.
Otis, George Jr. *Transformations: A documentary*. 2002 Available at http://www.youtube.com/watch?v=dBvxWl7jXr0 Accessed 1.09.08
Padilla, René C. *Misión integral: Ensayos sobre el reino y la iglesia*. Buenos Aires: Nueva Creación, 1986.
Phillips, David B. "Protestantism in Bolivia to 1952." MPhil Thesis, University of Calgary, 1968.
Platt, Tristan. 1988: "Pensamiento politico Aymara" in *Raices de America*, ed. Xavier Albó, 365-443. El mundo Aymara. Madrid: Alianza Editorial, 1988
Prado Meza, Amalia. *Dios es evangelista no? Un estudio comunicacional entre Collas evangelicos en Tierra de Cambas*. La Paz: Plural editores, 1997.
Romeiro, Paulo. *Decepcionados com a graça: Esperanças e frustrações no Brasil Neo-Pentecostal*. São Paulo: Editora Mundo Cristão, 2005.
Riviere, Gilles. "Bolivia: el Pentecostalismo en la sociedad Aymara del Altiplano." Pages 259-294 in *Gracias a Dios y a los Achachilas. Ensayos la sociología de la religión en los Andes*. Edited by Alison Spedding. La Paz: ISEAT, 2004.
Ruibal, Julio Cesar. *Ungido para la cosecha del tiempo final*. Miami: Editorial Vida, 1999.
Sagarnaga, Jedu A. *Diccionario de la cultura nativa en Bolivia*. La Paz: Producciones CIMA, 2002.
Sepúlveda, Juan. "Pentecostalism as popular religiosity" *International review of mission* vol 78, No 309: 80-88, 1989.
Spedding, Alison. *Religión en los Andes: Extirpación de idolatrías y modernidad de la fe andina*. La Paz: ISEAT, 2008.
Spedding, Alison, and Abraham Colque. *Vision del mundo, simbolismo y practicas andinas: Desafios para el Cristianismo*. La Paz: ISEAT, 2002.
Stoll, David. *Is Latin American Turning Protestant?* Berkeley: University of California Press, 1990.
Strobele-Gregor, Juliana. *Indios de piel blanca: Evangelistas fundamentalistas en Chuquiyawu*. La Paz: Hisbol, 1989.

Tancara, Juan J. *Teologia pentecostal: Propuesta desde comunidades Pentecostales de la ciudad del Alto*. La Paz: ISEAT, 2005.

Ticona Alejo, Esteban. ed. *Los Andes desde los Andes: Aymaranakana, Quichwanakana Yatxatawipa, Lup'iwipa*. La Paz: ediciones Yachaywasi, 2003.

Thomas, Nancy J. "Weaving the Word: Writing About God in Culturaly Appropiate ways." PhD Dissertation, Fuller Theological Seminary, 1998

Walls, Andrew F. The missionary movement in Christian history: Studies in the transformation of faith, New York: Orbis Books, 1996.

Willems, Emilio. *Followers of the New Faith: Culture Change and the Rise of Protestantism in Brazil and Chile*. Nashville: Vanderbilt University Press, 1967.

———. *Gospel and culture*, Willowbank Report (Bermudas: Lausanne occasional paper 2, 1978).

Wilson, Dwight J. 'Katrhryn Kuhlman (1907-76)' in the New Internationakl Dictionary of Pentecostal and Charismatic Movements: Revised and Expanded Edition, eds. Stanley Burgess and Eduard Van Der Mass, 826. Grand Rapids: Zondervan, 2003

Zúñiga, Eliseo. La gran conquista. Supertino: DIME, 1995.

Langham Literature and its imprints are a ministry of Langham Partnership.

Langham Partnership is a global fellowship working in pursuit of the vision God entrusted to its founder John Stott –

> ***to facilitate the growth of the church in maturity and Christ-likeness through raising the standards of biblical preaching and teaching.***

Our vision is to see churches in the Majority World equipped for mission and growing to maturity in Christ through the ministry of pastors and leaders who believe, teach and live by the word of God.

Our mission is to strengthen the ministry of the word of God through:
- nurturing national movements for biblical preaching
- fostering the creation and distribution of evangelical literature
- enhancing evangelical theological education

especially in countries where churches are under-resourced.

Our ministry

Langham Preaching partners with national leaders to nurture indigenous biblical preaching movements for pastors and lay preachers all around the world. With the support of a team of trainers from many countries, a multi-level programme of seminars provides practical training, and is followed by a programme for training local facilitators. Local preachers' groups and national and regional networks ensure continuity and ongoing development, seeking to build vigorous movements committed to Bible exposition.

Langham Literature provides Majority World preachers, scholars and seminary libraries with evangelical books and electronic resources through publishing and distribution, grants and discounts. The programme also fosters the creation of indigenous evangelical books in many languages, through writer's grants, strengthening local evangelical publishing houses, and investment in major regional literature projects, such as one volume Bible commentaries like *The Africa Bible Commentary* and *The South Asia Bible Commentary*.

Langham Scholars provides financial support for evangelical doctoral students from the Majority World so that, when they return home, they may train pastors and other Christian leaders with sound, biblical and theological teaching. This programme equips those who equip others. Langham Scholars also works in partnership with Majority World seminaries in strengthening evangelical theological education. A growing number of Langham Scholars study in high quality doctoral programmes in the Majority World itself. As well as teaching the next generation of pastors, graduated Langham Scholars exercise significant influence through their writing and leadership.

To learn more about Langham Partnership and the work we do visit **langham.org**

www.ingramcontent.com/pod-product-compliance
Lightning Source LLC
Chambersburg PA
CBHW050831160426
43192CB00010B/1982